To Do My Best

James E. West and the History of the Boy Scouts of America

Nide,
Regards

Edward L. Rowan, MD

Ed Rowan

PUBLISHING WORKS
EXETER, NH

Published by:
PublishingWorks, Inc.
60 Winter Street
Exeter, NH 03833
603-778-9883

Distributed by:
Revolution Booksellers
1-800-REV-6603

LCCN: 2005926233
ISBN: 1-933002-53-0
ISBN-13: 978-1-933002-53-8

Second Edition, 2007

To Judy

For supporting my magnum opus.

Contents

Acknowledgments

I am indebted to "Green Bar Bill" Hillcourt for the encouragement to write a book that he was unable to write.

I am particularly grateful to the members of the West family, especially his daughter Helen, grandsons James E. West III, and Bill Higgins and granddaughter Lynn Rasmussen and to the old-time Scouters who shared their memories with me.

Librarians and staff at the Library of Congress, Springfield College Library, Missouri Historical Society, American Jewish Archives, National Scouting Museum, and especially the Lawrence L. Lee Museum/Max I. Silber Scouting Library were very helpful.

Prof. John Phillips, Dr. Jack Dizer, Dr. Lynn Horne and Jim Ellis read the manuscript and offered critical comments.

The staff of PublishingWorks.

Thank you all very much.

Foreword

James E. West stands out as the most important figure in the history of the Boy Scout movement in the United States. He created the organization we know today. This book has been extraordinarily successful because Scouters want a true history that will enable them to understand the contemporary decision-making process. It is a loving critique from someone who has spent more than fifty years in the movement. Although West's administrative style was often viewed as harsh by his contemporaries, we honor his legacy that Scouting is, first and foremost, "for the boy."

—E.L.R.

Introduction

His grave in Valhalla, New York is untended. No one has asked for directions to it from the cemetery office in years. The stone itself has British emblems instead of the American ones he had designed to distinguish his organization from its English counterpart. His wife is buried at his side, despite her wish not to be there. He had cultivated his legacy very carefully. He ended in obscurity.

The man had been a crippled orphan, but, driven by ambition, he rose to head the largest youth organization in the free world. He knew seven presidents and was honored by another. He was on the cover of *Time* magazine.

He was described as the consummate organization man, an educator, and a leading progressive. He was also characterized as autocratic, chauvinistic, and racist. All of these terms have also been applied to the organization he once headed. He was James E. West and the organization is the Boy Scouts of America (BSA).

When West took over the BSA in 1911 there were 61,000 members, and when he retired thirty-two years later the organization had grown to over one and one-half million members and over ten million boys had been in the program. He established the policy, procedures, and philosophy that continue to dominate the program. Once a powerful presence, he is now largely forgotten. The Boy Scouts appear to want it that way.

Despite his historical importance, it has been extremely difficult to gather information about this man. When the national headquarters moved from New Jersey to Texas in 1979, the BSA microfilmed only nine of fifty-six boxes of West files, in no particular order, and still makes access difficult. One local Scout Executive insisted, "We have no history, only a future." The custodian of the records said, "My job is to protect our history from modern interpretation." Before the move, two researchers had access to records such as scrapbooks, minutes and stenographic transcripts.[1] More recent researchers have been told that the records were "lost" and no longer exist.[2] Apparently, the BSA once commissioned an official biography, but after it was completed, a person at national headquarters kept it "under lock and key and it will never see the light of day."

Long after West's death, an associate described him as "not a comfortable man to work with or for."[3] A very recent article in the Scouting literature refers to West as "prickly and hard to please" - a designation that those who knew him personally would have called an understatement.[4]

Who was this man? What did he do that requires a "cover-up?" Is there a "smoking gun" that, if discovered, will discredit the organization? West was very clearly a man of his time and he shared the attitudes and beliefs of his peers. He also established the organizational model that most non-profits use today. He brought order out of chaos and mediated among the powerful personalities who, if left to their own devices, would have destroyed the fledgling organization. He was the right man for the job.

As time went on, however, he and the Boy Scouts of America became synonymous in his own mind. As his version of history evolved, it became more dramatic and assigned him a greater role. He took personal charge of both tiny details and major decisions from reviewing the outgoing mail to telling Norman Rockwell how to paint a magazine cover. He was very proprietary about the "Scouts," fighting to have the Girl Scouts give up their name and resisting "Cub Scouts" as too young to be part of his program. In responding to a procedural question, he would have his stenographer take down his response, and it then became official policy. His domination of the central organization was so complete that there was no designated successor.

Powerful in office, he was, at the same time, a man with chronic illness and pain as well as family tragedy. For his official portrait, a smile had to be painted on because he seldom had one in real life. His daughter said, "The orphanage took all the joy out of his life."

West was a man of paradox. He presided over a strictly segregated organization but assigned all the Boy Scouts' share of the royalties from Irving Berlin's "God Bless America" Fund to "Negro Scouting." He did not believe that women were capable enough to participate in his Scouting Movement but he sent his daughters to Mount Holyoke and Vassar. He promoted the vision of the self-sufficient Scout but he himself never camped. The West family lived in a large home in New Rochelle, New York with a staff of three. He seems to have truly wanted to be liked, but he was apparently incapable of maintaining friendships or close relationships. He offered an open invitation to Scouts to write to him with their problems and questions, but if any ever did, the papers are in the forty-seven "lost" file boxes. He took pride in adding "Reverent" to the Scout Law and encouraged his Chief Scout Librarian in his efforts to stamp out the evil influence of pulp fiction. He also broke out a train window with his cane when the porter would not open it for him, and each day he made rounds in his office and used that cane to sweep clean any "untidy desk." He hoped that Scouts would think of him as "Uncle Jimmy." His staff called him that behind his back, but to his face he was always "Dr. West." The doctorate was honorary. He was universally respected, but not many people liked him.

James E. West overcame tremendous handicaps, and he truly believed in his mission to build character in the youth of America and to train them for citizenship. But did Scouting become an extension of West and his need to prove himself to the world? Did he really believe in the Movement for its own sake, or was it all about him? There is no statue of West, so, is the organization he created his monument? Has it changed much since he retired, or has it remained chiseled in granite? West's life was the embodiment of the American dream. He overcame childhood adversity and became very successful, but was his a model to emulate? As the centennial of the founding of American Scouting draws near in 2010, and as the Boy Scouts of America continues its struggle with the "Three G's," the issues of "God, girls, and gays," West's story is all the more relevant. It needs to be told.

Notes

[1] Carolyn Wagner and David Macleod
[2] William Hillcourt, personal communication
[3] Pote, Harold. *Fifty years of Scouting and its Pioneers.* Privately printed and undated, page 3
[4] *Boys' Life.* 1/2001, page 13

Chapter 1

The Early Years

James Edward West was born on May 16, 1876, at the Columbia Hospital, then at the corner of 25th and L Streets in Washington, D.C. His birth certificate lists his father as James Robert West, a "merchant from Tennessee" and his mother as Mary F. Tyri (later spelled Tyree) West, "seamstress", also from Tennessee.[1] It was her second pregnancy and first live birth. It was later reported that the Wests had descended from Pocahontas, but this was never documented, and West himself never claimed that lineage. (His eldest son's wife did, however, and this may have been the basis for the story.) In fact, after he became famous, West lamented that no one ever contacted him claiming to be a relative.[2]

His father was supposed to have died before West was born or shortly thereafter, but there is no death certificate on file in the District of Columbia. Perhaps he just moved on. If West even remembered his very early life with his mother, he never said or wrote anything about it. Mary West had tuberculosis, and when she was hospitalized on July 3, 1882, young Jimmy, age six, was placed in the Washington City Orphan Home at 14th and S Streets. According to Head, Jimmy was originally an institutional pet who lived with the matron's daughter; however, he was moved to the general population when his mother died later that year.[3] She was buried in the Greenland Cemetery. This cemetery was subsequently moved to make way for a public building. No records of the disposal of the bodies are known to exist.

At the orphanage, Jimmy complained of knee and hip pain. This was most apparent at the start of the workday and the staff thought that he was "shamming." Depending on the version of events, he was beaten with a stick, whipped, or starved to break his will. Someone must have taken his somatic complaints seriously, however, because on July 10, 1883 he was admitted to Providence Hospital with the diagnosis of tuberculosis. He spent much of the next year and a half in bed. His leg was strapped from his waist to the sole of his foot and a ten-pound weight was hung over the end of the bed.[4] He was once anesthetized in preparation for experimental surgery, but the physician changed his mind and the boy received no treatment other than immobilization. (Although it seems inadequate now, such immobilization was the treatment of choice at the time for "white swelling" or a tubercular joint.[5]) With one leg now shorter than the other as a result of the diseased hip joint, West was discharged as incurable on January 16, 1885. He was eight years old. In the 1930s, a potential biographer reviewed over twenty thousand Providence Hospital progress notes and found not a single one about young James West.[6] He received little attention while hospitalized and his sense of isolation must have been overwhelming. The orphanage initially refused to take him back because he was unable to work. The hospital apparently then dumped him with his bag and crutches on the doorstep, and the orphanage had no choice but to accept him. West's sense of rejection must have been overwhelming, as well.

After Jimmy returned to the orphanage, he was put to work caning chairs and sewing with the girls. He was bitter and felt unwanted, but the activity kept him from brooding. According to Head, "he realized the blessing of occupation. He had work to do and he quickly found the will and spirit to do it, and thus he kept his mind from brooding over his own handicaps and feeling sorry for himself. He began to realize his own ability, too. Though his limbs might be crippled, his hands were not, and by training them, he could accomplish something."[7] "I began to acquire faith in myself. In time, I said, 'I might be able to work my way up with my hands.'"[8] Providentially, Mrs. Ellis Spear, the wife of General Ellis Spear, the U.S. Patent Commissioner, visited him. She is identified as a "friend" of his mother but was, more likely, a former employer. She gave Jimmy a toy ox cart and books that her children had read. She took him on visits into her home and asked him about his reading. A new world opened up for him. He could develop his mind as well as his muscles.

He read voraciously and got up early to read the morning paper that was delivered to the orphanage. He then folded it carefully before the matron got it. He wanted to read more, but the orphanage library was locked. There was no access because the administrators worried that the children might damage the books. West then organized the other children and they covered over one thousand books with brown paper in order to protect them. West recounted later:

> My, what a lot of fun we had covering those books. And what a lot of work, too. Many of the children were as eager as I was to be able to use them and they all worked with a will, not only covering them, but marking and cataloging them too. There was an old Remington typewriter at the institution. I decided to use this for the cataloging work. But it was a pretty well-worn and dilapidated old machine that needed a lot of repair work. That did not stop me. Though I had never explored the mechanism of a typewriter, I tackled the job. I had unbounded confidence in my ability with my hands. I was training them to the point of ultimate dexterity. Indeed, in later years, I achieved proficiency in many manual arts, being able to wipe a joint as well as the best trained plumber could do it, or sew as well as any girl. Yes, I could make a button-hole or a broom; in fact, later I made all the brooms for the institution. But dismantling and repairing that typewriter was a mighty hard job. It took me three months to take it apart, clean it, and reassemble it. I learned everything there was to know about that machine, however, and in the end it served us well in our work of cataloging the books in the library.[9]

After the books were cataloged, West had to encourage the other children to read. "At first, I had to offer from my meager resources a cent for every book read and secure permission for those reading to remain up an extra hour each night."[10] Read they did. West had led his first major project to a successful conclusion.

By age twelve West decided that he needed to go to public school outside the orphanage. He had to convince the authorities that he could still do his chores and he was finally allowed to go. At the time, he was taking care of the furnaces, looking after a flock of 150 chickens, and doing the institutional laundry. He entered the fifth grade in public school. Twenty-four other orphans went to school with him. They probably wore the institutional blue jean uniform. West continued to read. "By the time I was 16, I had read, without exaggeration, every book on which I could get my hands - Cooper, Dickens, Scott, Gibbons *Decline and Fall of the Roman Empire* entire [sic], if you please, Macauley and Victor Hugo, Shakespeare and others. The institution routine made it necessary for me not only to read the Bible, but commit to memory many chapters and verses."[11] West had a single disciplinary problem when he was expelled briefly in the seventh grade. Classes had been let out to watch a circus parade, and Jimmy and his buddy, Fisher, had followed the parade to the circus grounds and not returned for afternoon classes. Both missed a test and received a failing grade. When West protested, he was expelled. His teacher, Miss Louise Connolly, came to his support because he had been loyal and not wanted to leave his friend. He was allowed to return to school and the education he was so desperate to receive.

Many years later, West commented on that school experience:

> For thirteen years, I was in an orphan's home, and one of the most disagreeable experiences I had was upon the numerous occasions when I was made conscious of the fact that I was different from other boys. I secured permission to go to the public school for the fifth grade. They have a law in the District of Columbia which permitted at that time the issuance of books to those who were in poverty. The mortification I felt on being asked to stand before the whole school, and having it driven home that the city was giving me my books, the mortification that came to me as I sat in the galleries of various churches on Sundays listening to the minister pray that a liberal collection be made in order that I might be clothed and fed—oh, that is very degrading to a boy. I have never forgotten it.[12]

After graduating from the eighth grade, and still on crutches, West decided to go to high school. First he had to convince the principal of Business High School, Alan Davis, to take him, and again he had to convince orphanage authorities that he could still do his work. He got up at 2 AM to do the laundry so that he could be done in time to go to classes. He also shoveled large quantities of coal to bank the furnaces for the night. He did everything well, finished the curriculum in two years, and graduated with honors in 1895. At Business High he started and edited the school newspaper, *The Balance Sheet*, studied and became proficient at shorthand, bookkeeping, and typing, acted as a substitute math teacher, and was business manager of the football team.

By the time he graduated, West had many other responsibilities at the orphanage and he received a small salary as well as his own room. He had progressed from being "big brother" to ninety younger boys to Junior Officer, directing work and recreational activities for the children. At one point, he organized the children to paint and whitewash the building. He also complained to the Board of Directors that the institution was spending more on meals for the fourteen staff members than on meals for the 180 children. A typical day's menu for the orphans was bread and milk for breakfast, water in which vegetables had been boiled for lunch, and bread and milk again for supper. The food situation was corrected, but West lost his job. In November 1896 he was twenty years old and out on his own.

"Young West was not at all dismayed. He says the first thing he did was to put an advertisement in the paper to coach boys in their studies. Two jobs were offered and he took them both. One paid him $20.00 and the other offered him room and board."[13]

He also found work in a bicycle shop. The shop owner, Mr. Von Beckman, had put a help wanted sign in the window, and West applied to be the bookkeeper.[14] The shop was an agency of the Victor Bicycle Company. At that time, the company had a rule that every employee, even bookkeepers, had to be able to ride a bicycle. Von Beckman could not be bothered with a cripple who could not ride, but West took up the challenge and rented a bicycle for fifty cents. "That was a horrible ordeal. For six hours I struggled to master that wheel. I had terrible falls. I was black, and blue, and cut. But I mastered it!"[15] That was Saturday; on Monday, he went back to the shop and demanded the job. He got it and, realizing that his crutches were a handicap to him in the impression that he made on others, he never used them again.

One thing that had become very obvious to West was that children were often the victims of rigid and capricious authority. He brooded about this injustice, and he wanted to be in a position to do something about it and to give children a chance. He thought he could best do it as a lawyer. He read law with an attorney, but the process was too slow so he applied to law school. Turned down by one law school, he persuaded the dean of National Law School in Washington to give him a chance. To support himself, West worked as an assistant to the Secretary of the YMCA. He was also appointed guardian of two younger boys from the orphanage and they lived with him. He dropped out of law school for the year 1898 to serve as General Secretary for the YMCA when the regular Secretary went off to serve in the Spanish American War. It was here he furthered his reputation as a person who could take charge and get things done.

The wing of the YMCA building in which night school classes were held burned down, and the school had to be closed. The Board had no money to reopen but West urged them to let him try. As he later said, "I didn't ask for money, I asked for permission to go ahead." He convinced the teachers to return without pay and the builders to donate time and materials and defer some payments until the school was functioning again on a paying basis. When the school did reopen, it had 200 students instead of the 136 it had when it closed.

West returned to Law School in 1899, attending classes at night and working as a clerk in the War Department during the day. That year, he became one of the three founders of the Business High School Alumni Association, whose goals were not only to secure jobs for alumni but also to lobby Congress for a new building.

After receiving his LLB in 1900, West went on to earn an LLM in 1901. That year, he was admitted to the bar in the District of Columbia and in 1902 to the Court of Appeals. (In 1906 he was admitted to the bar of the Supreme Court but it is not known whether he ever argued a case there.) In 1902, President Theodore Roosevelt appointed West as the attorney member (he was called a Judge) of the Board of Pension Appeals in the Interior Department. His salary was $2,000 per year. He later served as an Assistant Attorney in the Interior Department.

Outside of work, West was Superintendent of Sunday School for the Mount Pleasant Congregational Church where, over his five years in charge, attendance rose from three hundred to over one thousand. He joined the Masons and the Knights of Pythias and from 1904 to 1906 was Finance Chair of the United Boys Brigade of America. He began his tenure with the Washington Playground Association in 1906, first as a volunteer, but after 1908, as the paid secretary. The Association goal was to get better playgrounds for the children in Washington. In pursuit of this goal, West approached Roosevelt to use the White House grounds for ball games and lobbied Congress for appropriations. He succeeded in both endeavors. He later successfully organized a "Button Day" and sold buttons with a picture of President Taft saying, "I am for playgrounds."

Early in his legal career, West had his car stolen. West had left his two-seater parked while he visited a settlement house. He returned to find it gone. The police picked up the boy who stole it and West was asked to testify in court. When he learned that the boy had no lawyer, West volunteered to defend him. "Freddie" had been charged with driving without a license. If he were found guilty, the penalty would be imprisonment. West himself testified that he was still carrying the keys to the car and that Freddie had sat behind the wheel while other boys pushed the car. Technically, then, he was not driving. West won.[16] West firmly believed that children like Freddie should not be tried as adults. He believed that these cases should be heard in a different setting by personnel who knew how to deal with children. He helped organize a Citizens' Committee for Juvenile Court, lobbied Congress, and saw the first Judicial Court bill passed on March 12, 1906.[17] There was some support for West to be appointed the first judge, but this was not to be. Roosevelt had a different political appointment to make, but he assured West that he owed him a favor.

Theodore Dreiser, editor of *Delineator*, a New York magazine, had organized the National Child Rescue League. Its mission was "a home for every child and a child in every home." West served as Secretary of the League, and successfully placed over two thousand orphans in adoptive homes. As part of his ongoing interest in orphans, West called in the favor from Roosevelt and encouraged him to call a White House Conference on Dependent Children in January 1909. One story has it that he got into the White House while Roosevelt was being shaved and told his captive audience that if he could call for a conference on natural resources he could call for a conference on children. Roosevelt agreed. West served as Secretary. The final report recommended that all children be cared for in family homes or, if in temporary institutions, be housed in cottages with fewer than twenty-five children in each. Children should have access to education, facilities should have oversight by trained inspectors, and standards should be set by a Federal Children's Bureau. All of these points would have been dear to West, who could only have wished that they had been in place thirty years before. The Conference brought the problem of childcare to national attention and, for the first time, put West on the national stage. It also established a relationship with Roosevelt that would last a decade. West had great respect and affection for a man who, like himself, had overcome childhood handicaps. Roosevelt similarly admired the emphasis on self-reliance and character development that West embodied. After the conference, Theodore Roosevelt sent West an oft-quoted thank you note: "But for you there would have been no conference. I have always thought well of you, but now I feel you are one of those disinterested and patriotic citizens to whom this country stands under a particular debt of gratitude."[18] "With all these activities, and the amazing results he achieved, he was fast gaining recognition as a social worker with vision, boundless energy, and the ability to achieve the almost impossible."[19] (West went on to participate in three more White House Conferences on Youth, for Harding in 1922, Hoover in 1930, and Franklin Roosevelt in 1940. None were to be as important to him as the first one.)

On June 19, 1907, West married Marion Speaks of Washington. She had been born in 1885, the daughter of Charles and Mary Speaks. Little is known about her family background. Her father was a government official, she had an older brother, and she was a teacher. She had been one of West's Sunday School teachers at the Mount Pleasant Congregational Church. On Christmas Day, 1909 James Ellis West was born. Unfortunately, West had lost his job in the Interior Department with the change in Administration and he now had a family to support. Although he still had his job with the Playground Association, West sent out notices in 1910 for the opening of a private law office in the Metropolitan Bank Building.

He never moved into that office because a man he had not met before, Colin Livingstone, a Washington banker, offered him a job as Managing Secretary of the newly organized Boy Scouts of America. It must have been a hard sell. "At first when the telephone invitation came for me to call upon Mr. Livingstone I was indifferent; although active in work for youth, I was not very much impressed with the thought of a new movement for boys; and it took a second and third invitation to bring us together, and I remember that when I responded and met with him for the first time, it required a good deal of salesmanship on his part to persuade me that it would be worthwhile for me to come over to New York and seriously consider what he had in mind."[20] West agreed to take the job for six months. The first office was in the YMCA building in New York City. West moved to New York and left his young family in Washington.

Notes

[1] District of Columbia # 7202, copy in BSA Archives

[2] Stearns, Myron, "Boys will be Scouts" *American Magazine* 6/27

[3] Head, Walter, "The boyhood ambition that built *Boys' Life*" *Boys' Life* 3/36, page 55

[4] Larkin W. Glazebrook, MD letter in BSA Archives

[5] See Webb, Gerald, *Tuberculosis.* New York: Hoeber, 1936

[6] Westhoff in BSA Archives

[7] Head page 55

[8] Stearns

[9] Head page 56

[10] West, James E. *Boys' Life* 11/33 page 20

[11] Ibid

[12] Proceedings of the 7th National Training Conference, 1939, page 355

[13] Head page 57

[14] Letter in BSA Archives

[15] Head page 57

[16] Stearns

[17] This, the beginning of the Juvenile Court system was the subject of a "You Are There" television episode in the 1950's.

[18] West, James E. *Making the Most of Yourself.* New York: Appleton-Century, 1941, page xiv

[19] Head page 57

[20] *Scouting.* 7/25 page 11

Chapter 2

The Run-up

A great deal had happened in Scouting before West came on the scene in January, 1911. Although many men had played important roles, five stand out: Robert S.S. Baden-Powell, Ernest Thompson Seton, Daniel Carter Beard, William D. Boyce, and Edgar M. Robinson. It is also important to understand the societal trends in the early part of the 20th Century that were so important to the shaping and success of the Scouting movement.

Baden-Powell

Robert Stephenson Smyth Baden-Powell was born in London, England on February 22, 1857.[1] His father died when "Stephe" was three. As a boy at Charterhouse School he delighted in avoiding the masters by going off into the woods. As a young Army officer, he integrated some of his outdoor skills into the structure and discipline of military life. A tireless self-promoter, Baden-Powell wrote books about his travels and experiences and illustrated them himself. In 1884 he wrote *Reconnaissance and Scouting* and in 1895 *Aids to Scouting for N.C.O.s and Men.* He used "Scouting" in the military sense of forward observation and the necessity of self-sufficiency. In 1896 he spent time with the American frontier "Scout" Frederick Burnham who was then working for the British Army in Africa. Baden-Powell admired Burnham's skills very much.[2] Baden-Powell rose through the ranks and in 1899 was sent to South Africa in the campaign against the Boers. A Colonel, he commanded the Frontier Force and (some say foolishly) found himself surrounded and under siege by the Boers at a town called Mafeking.

The Run-Up

Mafeking made Baden-Powell a hero. He sent regular dispatches to the London papers to keep his countrymen aware of his situation. As part of town administration, his staff organized a Cadet Corps of boys to provide messenger service throughout the siege. After 217 days, Mafeking was relieved on May 17, 1900. Without much other good news from the Cape Colony, this was the cause of great rejoicing throughout England. "B-P" was now a popular hero as attested to by the deluge of commemorative ceramics, pins, banners, and other memorabilia produced in his honor. Even before the war was over, B-P was assigned to develop a police force, the South African Constabulary. When he returned to England in 1903, he was appointed Inspector General of Cavalry.

As a recognized hero, B-P was often called upon for advice to the youth of the Empire. He was aware that young men who had grown up in urban poverty were not good military material. They had no practical outdoor skills and they did not recognize authority. He sincerely wanted to do something to improve the character of boys, so that when he learned that many boys were reading his *Aids to Scouting*, he decided to revise his concepts and develop a comprehensive scheme for boy training. He borrowed from several sources and completed his manuscript in 1907.

B-P wanted to test his scheme on boys before committing the program to publication, so he brought a group of twenty-two boys to Brownsea Island, Dorset for the first week of August 1907. He recruited about half the boys through army friends and half through the Boy's Brigade, a Christian youth group that emphasized military training. The whole spectrum of the British class system was represented. Each evening, B-P told a story about the use of a skill; the next morning, he taught that skill; in the afternoon, the boys played a game utilizing what they had been taught. He thought the whole scheme a success, and the first of six fortnightly parts of *Scouting for Boys* appeared on January 15, 1908. His publisher decided that he could generate more excitement by releasing a section every two weeks. The entire book was published on May 1.

The Boy Scout scheme became wildly popular with boys who quickly adopted the uniform consisting of the broad-brimmed hat of the South African Constabulary, Burnham's neck scarf, shorts, stave, and the Scout badge. Structure and organization became necessary and, in 1910 Lieutenant-General Baden-Powell retired to work full-time promoting and administering Scouting throughout Britain, the Empire, and the World. Many groups, including YMCAs, obtained *Scouting for Boys* from England and used the program in the United States.

Seton

Ernest Thompson was born in Durham, England on August 14, 1860 but the family emigrated to Canada in 1866.[3] When his father beat him, young Thompson retreated to the woods, animal study, and drawing. His later art training included a scholarship to the Royal Academy in London. When his father demanded that he be repaid for all services rendered since birth, Ernest did so. Then he rejected his father and changed his name to Seton. In 1881 he became naturalist for the Province of Manitoba and his fascination with wolves began. In 1883 he moved to New York to pursue a career as a naturalist-artist-writer. His early books - *Wild Animals I Have Known, Biography of a Grizzly*, and *Lives of the Hunted* - were all very successful. Seton's material was very popular and, in 1902, the *Ladies' Home Journal* asked him to provide a series of articles on woodcraft for boys. These were gathered together and, after a few editions as *The Red Book* or *How to Play Injun*, finally emerged as *The Birchbark Roll of the Woodcraft Indians* in 1906. Seton shared his work with Baden-Powell in a series of letters and a visit to London that same year.

Seton invited boys from around his home in Cos Cob, Connecticut to take part in his outdoor program and he eventually developed the Woodcraft League. This consisted of local tribes of boys who practiced woodcraft skills in the context of a romanticized Indian theme. Many YMCA summer camps used *The Birchbark Roll* as part of their program.

Beard

Daniel Carter Beard was born in Cincinnati, Ohio on June 21, 1850. His father and older brothers, artists all, left for New York City for greater opportunity when Dan was a teen-ager. He stayed behind in Ohio. Like Seton, he too spent his childhood wandering in the woods, sketching, and inventing things. He was imbued with a frontier sense of individualism and patriotism, as well as a strong sense of Christian morality.[4] As a young man, he traveled around the country as an engineer and surveyor and relaxed by sketching local animals. At the age of 34, he went to New York City to study art. There he began to write youth-oriented articles for *St. Nicholas* magazine based upon his own childhood activities. He collected these and other handicraft articles as the *American Boy's Handy Book* in 1882. Beard had joined the Art Student League in 1880. Seton met him there in 1883 and considered him a friend. Mark Twain asked him to illustrate his books.

In 1905, Beard became editor of *Recreation* magazine and, in July of that year, launched the Sons of Daniel Boone. The aim of this organization was to introduce boys to nature and to instill the spirit of the pioneers in them. Beard devised a structure of local "Forts" or "Stockades" with officers and program ideas taken from the magazine. Financial problems at *Recreation* caused him to leave in 1906, but his monthly column about the Sons of Daniel Boone ran for the next three years in *Woman's Home Companion*. There he developed a series of "Top Notch" awards named after and with the consent of popular icons such as President Roosevelt, Admiral Dewey, and Buffalo Bill Cody. After a conflict with the new female editor of *Woman's Home Companion*, Beard moved his column to the *Pictorial Review* in 1909. *Woman's Home Companion* retained the rights to the name "Sons of Daniel Boone", so Beard had to change the organization's name to Boy Pioneers. The program was the same. As before, each Fort reported directly to Beard who, by that time, dressed in buckskins and acted like a frontier sage. Unlike Scouting and Woodcraft, Beard's program had limited appeal to local YMCAs.

Boyce

William D. Boyce was born near New Texas, Pennsylvania on June 16, 1858.[5] After brief tries at teaching and college, he settled into the newspaper business. He owned *The Commercial* in Winnipeg, Manitoba and then the *Lisbon Clipper* in the Dakota Territory. In 1886 he joined Chicago printer Richard Donnelley to form the Mutual Newspaper Publishing Company that provided over two hundred subscribing newspapers with pre-set or pre-printed ads and articles. Boyce then got the idea to establish a nationally distributed rural and small town weekly.

The *Saturday Blade* was a family-oriented paper sold for five cents by boys who got to keep two and one-half cents for themselves. With this huge network of young salesmen, the *Blade* became the largest selling weekly newspaper in the country. Boyce soon acquired the *Chicago Ledger* and became involved in numerous business ventures that made him a very wealthy man. He also enjoyed hunting, fishing, and sailing and wrote books about his travels.

Boyce was a racist. He wrote approvingly of New Zealand's policy of "white only" immigration "to keep it free from the taint of coloured races."[6] He liked the neat white porters on Australian trains, "not crap-shooting negroes as on American trains."[7] He noted in South Africa that "it [black labor] is worthless except in the mines and Boer farms where only animal intelligence is needed."[8] "I could hardly believe that white women were nursing diseased negroes in this hospital until I saw them at work."[9] Boyce speculated that after the minerals ran out, "then the heart of Africa will return to its primeval condition, the happy home of the naked negro."[10]

On one of his adventures, Boyce encountered Scouting. The official version of this encounter was first put forth by West in his "Historical statement concerning the early development of the Boy Scouts of America."[11] He delivered this lecture to all National Training Schools and it was later published in the *Scoutmaster's Handbook*. According to this version, Boyce became lost in foggy London streets while on his way to keep a business appointment. A uniformed boy approached and asked if he could be of service. After the boy had shown him to his destination, Boyce offered him a tip. The boy refused, saying that he was a Scout and was simply doing a good turn. Boyce questioned the boy about the Scouts, and, after his appointment, the waiting boy took him to the Scouts' office on Henrietta Street. There he spent the entire afternoon talking with Baden-Powell. Impressed by this new organization, Boyce returned to the United States with a trunk full of "insignia, literature, and uniforms" and incorporated the Boy Scouts of America.[12]

Boyce recalled the events a bit differently in a February 27, 1928 letter to West.[13] Boyce wrote that in August 1909 he was enroute to British East Africa and Uganda on a photography and shooting expedition. He was standing in front of the Savoy Hotel in London wondering whether or not he should cross the busy street when a boy offered to help him across. The boy refused a tip because he was "a B-P Boy Scout." Boyce was curious; the boy gave him directions to the office; Boyce picked up a copy of *Scouting for Boys*. He read it during his four months in Africa and came back through London on his way home. He returned to the scout office and discussed with "whoever was in charge" the possibility of organizing in the United States and Canada. "Whoever was in charge" suggested that he limit his efforts to the United States and that if he were "on the level," the official material would be released to him. The man also said that it had been a mistake by the British not to have incorporated at the outset and that the Americans should have their own hero as Baden-Powell was unknown there. Boyce certainly knew who Baden-Powell was by 1928 and the man with whom he spoke was not he. There is not a word in Boyce's account about fog or a trunk full of materials. What is clear is that Boyce was truly impressed by that British scout. "The intense earnestness with which that good turn was done by that lad of twelve really caused him to take hold of this thing and give it a boost."[14]

After Boyce returned to the United States, he went to his friend Joe Cannon, the Speaker of the House to see about a Federal Charter for the Scouts. HB24747 was introduced but in the face of considerable fighting in the House over the chartering of the Rockefeller Foundation, the Scout bill was withdrawn. Boyce then decided to incorporate in the District of Columbia, and on February 8, 1910 the Boy Scouts of America came into being. Boyce now had an organization, but he didn't know what to do with it.

Robinson

Edgar M. Robinson was born in St. Stephen, New Brunswick in 1867.[15] He was an early volunteer in boys' work, running evangelical Protestant camps and conferences. He came to the United States to attend the YMCA's Springfield Training School and to be the half-time Boys' Secretary for the Massachusetts Department in 1898. By 1900 he was the first Secretary for the International Department (United States and Canada) for the YMCA and his office was in New York City. Robinson focused on adolescence as the prime time for character building activities and on the recruitment and training of men who would serve as local Boys' Secretaries. He emphasized a balance of activities and religious work. The YMCA was, and still is, building centered. Robinson was always looking for ways to get boys into his buildings in order to get their attention and mold their character. For Robinson and YMCA leaders throughout the world, the Boy Scout scheme was an ideal way to do that. Many local secretaries were using B-P's manual and forming troops as early as 1908. "We found scoutcraft to be a most excellent thing for our camps."[16] YMCA camps had begun around 1882 with "evangelistic and outing features to have been uppermost and well conducted." Camp was "a valuable feature of summer work with boys. Two results may thereby be obtained or at least promoted. First, a very intimate acquaintance will be developed by the leader with the dispositions of the boys with whom he is to work. Second, the boys themselves will be taught that pleasure-seeking does not necessitate any relaxation of Christian study and work, and that a full enjoyment of a vacation Sabbath does not imply any license, or forgetfulness of God's claim."[17]

To summarize then, by early 1910 Baden-Powell Scouts were organized in Britain and Canada and William Boyce held the rights to Scouting in the United States. Seton had his Woodcraft League and Beard his Boy Pioneers. Robinson and the YMCA ran summer camps and used some elements of all the other programs as part of their out-door activities.

Getting Together

J. A. Van Dis, the YMCA Boys' Work Secretary for Michigan, had begun organizing Scout troops based on *Scouting for Boys* in 1909. In February 1910 he read in the Chicago papers that Boyce had incorporated the Boy Scouts of America, and he quickly brought this to Robinson's attention.[18] Robinson traveled to Chicago, where he explained to Boyce that "we represented a movement that had many local organizations and both State and National supervision, and were in a position to promote his movement if he cared to cooperate."[19] Robinson appears to have been the first American to refer to Scouting as a "movement." In this context, a "movement" was dynamic and goal-directed, not static like an "organization." Boys and men were to participate in a movement, not simply belong to an organization. Boyce accepted the suggestion of the YMCA men and then did what he did best - pledged money ($1000 per month for a year) to support the organization. Then he left for a trip to South America. Boyce may have made as many as four contributions. (Seton said three.) According to Robinson, "Mr. Boyce's partner [Col. Hunter] did not think that Mr. Boyce was given enough publicity in connection with the Boy Scout organization for he had sent photographs to Mr. Robinson to be published and these were not published and little was said about Mr. Boyce in relation to the Boy Scout movement. Mr. Robinson had been advised to take this course due to the fact that Mr. Boyce having been recently divorced and there being a number of rumors in connection herewith. Mr. Boyce returned and refused to further support the organization."[20]

After his initial meeting with Boyce, Robinson returned to New York to begin the organizational process. He sent letters to boys' workers all over the country looking for potential members for a national organization. Meanwhile, William Randolph Hearst, publisher of the *New York American*, had incorporated the American Boy Scouts, Col. Peter S. Bomus headed the Boy Scouts of the United States, Col. E. S. Cornell the National Highway Patrol Association Scouts, and Col. William Verbeck the National Scouts of America. All were militaristic in nature. The members wore uniforms and drilled. Some carried guns. All the principals including Seton and Beard, but not Hearst, met with Robinson and other YMCA officials in a series of meetings in New York City in the Spring of 1910. Bomus and Verbeck merged their organizations into the Boy Scouts of America and took positions within it. Cornell folded his group as did Beard. Seton put the Woodcraft League on hold. Only the Hearst organization refused to recognize the Boy Scouts of America as the national movement and it was six more years before they capitulated. Robinson always believed that the *New York American* enjoyed name recognition in "American Boy Scouts."

Societal Changes

All these men shared a common goal - to develop character in boys. There was a general feeling in the early years of the twentieth century that immigration, movement into the cities, and the loss of the frontier had weakened the youth of America. In the good old days boys had to work hard and learn to be self-sufficient. This led to pride in themselves and, ultimately, to pride in America. The call for return to a hardier existence was put forth in such diverse ways as Seton's 1903 book, *Two Little Savages,* and psychologist G. Stanley Hall's recapitulation theory. According to Hall, adolescents had to pass through the culturally earlier savage stage before entering noble, civilized manhood. To youth workers, this meant that the youths' baser instincts had to be worked out through active, supervised recreation.[21] As Henry Curtis wrote in the *Educational Review* in 1916: "For nearly a generation there has been a feeling in certain educational circles that there was need that every boy should have an opportunity to live thru [sic] the race life, pursue the primitive industries and occupations and finally come to the civilization of the 20th century by much the same stages that the race has followed . . . [M]ost of the delinquency of our cities was much the breaking out of the normal savagery which lies at the basis of the character of every normal boy, but which was finding no expression under the unnatural conditions of the city."[22]

The principal reason for this move to urban areas had been the industrialization of America. With industrialization came tycoons, bosses, trusts, tariffs, factory girls, and child labor. This spawned the Progressive Movement. According to Hofstader, "The Progressive movement, then, may be looked upon as an attempt to develop the moral will, the intellectual insight, and the political and administrative agencies to remedy the accumulated evil and negligence of the period of industrial growth."[23] In 1912 the Progressive Party platform argued that "social evils will not remedy themselves and it is wrong to sit by passively and wait for time to take care of them. People of the country should be stimulated to work energetically to bring about social progress."[24] This approach was consistent with the views of so-called "social Christianity" as a way to actively solve the moral problems of urban degeneration secondary to industrialization. Progressives saw that social progress had to begin in childhood. They wanted not only physical development through outdoor activity but also educational opportunities and an emphasis on civic concern for all.[25]

A related, although unacknowledged, common belief was that such solid middle-class Protestant values were the ideal to which all should strive. Progressive reform would lead not only to moral reform but also to an organized society and to social control. The Scout scheme addressed both concerns, as it provided rigorous outdoor activity and a code of conduct for community living. According to Curtis:

> It would appear that scouting corresponds with a fundamental interest of boys; that it holds in solution the essential virtues of adolescence with its thirst for manliness and achievement and heroism; that it gives health and endurance and hardihood on the physical side, companionableness on the social side, alertness and resourcefulness on the mental side, and the appropriate virtues of the period on the moral side. Scouting is something that every boy should have. It develops manliness and virtue where the school develops the intellect. The two are supplementary to each other. The boy scouts train in the old racial activities and virtues, the schools in the latest acquisitions of the race.[26]

Scouting came on the scene as these societal changes and social reactions were evolving. It was successful because it added something special. Levy thought that there were five key elements in this. There was the romance of the out-of-doors and the ability to acquire distinctive symbols and insignia for competence in outdoor activity. The program emphasized good citizenship. It was democratic and peaceful. Leaders were men of prestige and influence, and the leadership aggressively promoted Scouting to a place of national significance.[27] These elements came together at the right time in history, and the Scout Movement was poised for success.

Open For Business

On June 1, 1910 Robinson opened the BSA office in the YMCA at 124 E 28 Street in New York City.[28] John Alexander, the YMCA Boys' Work Secretary from Philadelphia, was hired as the first managing secretary and he had one stenographer. The first organizational meeting was held on June 21. Seton and Beard were there. As the only man present whose name had been on the bill Boyce had introduced in Congress, Colin Livingstone, President of the American National Bank in Washington, D.C. was elected temporary chairman. Seton was rewriting B-P's manual but William Murray, chair of that project, later complained that he had to rewrite the rewritten material because it was addressed to adults and not to boys.[29]

The committee also authorized an experimental camp at Silver Bay, New York for the last two weeks in August. This had already been organized as a YMCA camp and was comprised of twenty groups of seven boys each from twenty different cities. Beard and Robinson were there briefly, but Seton was in charge, and it was, in reality, a Tribe of Woodcraft gathering.

During the fall of 1910, the Committee on Organization (Seton as Chair, Lee Hammer, George Pratt, Luther Gulick, Jacob Riis, Robinson, Livingstone, Beard, Verbeck, and Bomus) formed a National Council. The movement became operational on October 25, 1910 under a newly accepted Constitution and By-Laws. Livingstone became president of the newly named Executive Board. Seton became Chief Scout. Alexander had asked to be relieved of his duties in order to devote full time to writing manuals, so Robinson assumed the role of managing secretary while the search for a permanent secretary was initiated.

On November 2, 1910 Ernest Bicknell, National Director of the American Red Cross and a Board Member of the Washington Playground Association, wrote to Luther Gulick, president of the Playground Association of America, a member of the Russell Sage Foundation and the Committee on Organization, to recommend his Secretary, James E. West for the job as managing secretary. "West is one of the most resourceful, energetic, and indefatigable men whom I have seen in social work. He seems thoroughly businesslike in the matter of expenditures, accounting, and all those business details which are so often burdensome and neglected by people in social work."[30] Robinson asked Livingstone in Washington to make inquiries. West later said that he had been "number one" on three different lists. According to Robinson, William Knowles Cooper of the District of Columbia YMCA made the second recommendation.[31] The third was from the Charity Organization Society.[32] West was initially reluctant, but after traveling to New York City to meet the Board, he agreed to serve. Baden-Powell wrote to Robinson, "I am delighted to hear that Mr. West is to be secretary. I feel that under his guidance the movement ought to go ahead on very sound grounds."[33]

Notes

1 See Hillcourt, William, *Baden-Powell: Two Lives of a Hero.* New York: G.P. Putnam's Sons, 1964

2 Baden-Powell, R.S.S. *Matabele Campaign 1896.* London: Metheun, 1897

3 See Seton, E.T. *Trail of an Artist Naturalist.* New York: Scribners, 1940

4 See Whitmore, Allan, *Beard, Boys, and Buckskins.* Unpublished PhD dissertation Northwestern University, 1970

5 See Petterchak, J. *Lone Scout: W. D. Boyce and American Boy Scouting.* Legacy Press, 2003

6 Boyce, W. D. *Illustrated Australia and New Zealand.* Chicago: Rand McNally, 1922. Page 235

7 Ibid, page 209

8 Boyce, W. D. *Illustrated Africa.* Chicago: Rand McNally, 1925. Page 674

9 Ibid page 595

10 Ibid page 383

11 West, James E. Historic statement of the Boy Scouts of America. BSA mimeo, 1931

12 See, for example, Oursler, Will, *The Boy Scout Story.* Garden City, NY: Doubleday & Co. 1955

13 Letter in BSA Archives

14 West in Proceedings of the 2nd National Training Conference, 1922, page 27

15 See Macleod, David, *Building Character in the American Boy.* Madison: University of Wisconsin Press, 1983, page 118 ff

16 11/07/17 letter to West in Robinson Archives at Springfield College (EMR Archives)

17 Robinson, E. A. *The Early Years.* New York: Association Press, 1950, Page 77

18 Murray, W. *The History of the Boy Scouts of America.* New York: BSA, 1937, page 24

19 1948 note in EMR Archives

20 7/07/17 letter in EMR Archives

21 Macleod page 99

22 Curtis, "The Boy Scouts" in *Educational Review* 12/15 page 495

23 Hofstader, *The Progressive Movement 1910-1915.* Englewood Cliffs, NJ: Prentice Hall, 1963 page 3

24 Ibid page 5

25 Gornick, Thomas, "James E. West: A servant of youth" unpublished manuscript 1973, page 19

26 Curtis, page 507

27 Levy,H. *Building a Popular Movement.* New York: Russell Sage Foundation, 1944 p. 21

28 Murray, page 28

29 Murray, Wm. *As He Journeyed.* New York: Association Press, 1929 page 348

30 Letter in BSA Archives

31 EMR Archives

32 West, Historic statement page 8

33 Letter in BSA Archives

Chapter 3

The First Five Years

On January 2, 1911, James E. West opened the new office of the Boy Scouts of America at 200 Fifth Avenue in New York City. He had a staff of seven. Bicknell's recommendation had touted West as an organized man. He was. The amount of work must have been staggering. Sixty councils were organized in the first month of the year, and over fifty scoutmasters were being commissioned each month. By May there were thirty-five employees in the office. During the year, the office processed 198,439 pieces of mail.

As membership in the BSA grew rapidly, the Executive Board turned to refining the scheme and making the program less British and more American. The first step was to revise Seton's version of Baden-Powell's handbook. The second printing in 1910 eliminated all Baden-Powell's specific references to Britain and temporarily left eleven blank pages headed "Scoutmaster's memoranda." To complete the 1911 revision, the Executive Board then appointed four commissions:

1. Standardization of the Scout Oath, Law, and advancement procedures
2. Finance
3. Badges, awards, and equipment
4. Permanent organization and field supervision.

West was a member of each commission. He was a very persuasive man. His daughter would later describe him as "dynamic, forceful and persistent but low key."[1] If he believed in something strongly enough,

West would repeatedly present his point of view from a variety of perspectives until he got his way. This was evident in the final product of each commission and in institutional decisions throughout his tenure.

Scout Oath and Law

Baden-Powell based his "Scout Promise" on the "code of the Knights of the Middle Ages."[2]

> On my honour I promise that I will do my best,
> To do my duty to God and the King,
> To help other people at all times,
> To obey the Scout Law.

West prevailed over Beard in calling the American version an "Oath" rather than a "Vow" and expanded the third part in keeping with his goal of character development. He essentially paraphrased the YMCA mission "to put Christian principles into practice through programs that build healthy spirit, mind and body for all."

> On my honor I will do my best,
> To do my duty to God and my Country and to obey
> the Scout Law;
> To help other people at all times;
> To keep myself physically strong, mentally awake,
> and morally straight.

The British Scout Law had nine parts: A Scout's Honour is to be Trusted, "A Scout is Loyal to the King, and to his officers, and to his parents, his country, and his employers. He must stick to them through thick and thin against anyone who is their enemy or who even talks badly of them." A Scout's Duty is to be Useful and Help Others, A Scout is a Friend to All, and a Brother to Every Other Scout no Matter to What Social Class the Other Belongs, A Scout is Courteous, A Scout is a Friend to Animals, A Scout Obeys orders, A Scout Smiles and Whistles, A Scout is Thrifty.

After rejecting multiple suggestions by Seton, the Americans added just three more. According to West:

We agreed finally to add one for cleanliness which the English did not have. We added one for bravery. They did not have this. My judgment of the Twelfth Scout Law [Reverent] is that it is one of the very finest things in the whole scheme of Scouting and one of the reasons we have had such outstanding success. It is one of the reasons we have such a large percentage of boys. From my point of view, the real people in America, the people that have made America from the early days, are those who have had deep religious convictions based upon personal religious experiences and those who serve others because of the joy of service. I felt at that time, as I feel now, that there is nothing more essential in the education of the youth in America than to give them religious instruction and I advocated that this be included in the Twelfth Scout Law, A Scout is Reverent."[3]

Closely related was Article III of the Constitution: "The Boy Scouts of America maintains that no boy can grow into the best kind of citizenship without recognizing his obligation to God."

For West, this was very personal.

I had grown into manhood with one outstanding source of power and guidance. I had been very fortunate in having been led into a very deep and strong religious conviction; and whatever I did, may I hope that it may always be so, I was guided by a conviction that I was here on earth with obligations to serve, and obligations to serve in accordance with the teachings of Jesus Christ.

Men, you and I know that our movement stands for religious training in its principles of organization, and because of our record of its administration; it is our privilege to be servants, or leaders if you prefer it, in one of the greatest organizations the world has yet seen for the advancement of the Kingdom of God through a program for character development and citizenship training under conditions which challenge the very best that is within us.[4]

West was to return to this theme again and again, as he often said that this religious emphasis was his greatest contribution to the movement.

Among other changes to the British Law was the elimination of Loyalty to employer because unions objected. Friendship to all social classes was dropped because America was not perceived to have such classes. Americans would not follow the British tradition and pour a mug of cold water down an offender's sleeve if the Scout swore instead of smiling and whistling. The result was a simplified American Scout Law: A Scout is Trustworthy, Loyal, Helpful, Friendly, Courteous, Kind, Obedient, Cheerful, Thrifty, Brave, Clean, Reverent. In 1912 the British added "A Scout is Clean in Thought, Word, and Deed" as their tenth Scout Law. They never adopted Brave or Reverent.

The concept of a Good Deed was taken from the third Law, a Scout is Helpful, where "he must do at least one good turn to someone each day." "Do A Good Turn Daily" became the slogan of the BSA. For a motto, Baden-Powell's "Be Prepared," was chosen over Seton's "Be Ready," Beard's "Be Steadfast," or Beard's second choice of Davy Crockett's, "Be sure you're right, then go ahead." Beard thought "Be Prepared" was a "war phrase" and "mongrel Latin." Baden-Powell would later explain that "the slogan of the Scout is 'Be Prepared.' This was adopted, with much of the uniform, from the South African Constabulary. The men of this force chose that motto for themselves partly because it spoke of their readiness to take on any kind of duty at any time, and also because it brought in my initials. In heraldry it is customary for the motto of a coat-of-arms to contain some play upon the name of the owner and the motto is generally drawn on a scroll beneath the arms."[5]

Finance

At a meeting on February 14, 1911 at the Willard Hotel in Washington, D.C., the Finance Commission recommended that "no general canvas should be made for financial support - but that a number of the friends of the Movement, from various parts of the country, should be called upon to care for its financial needs during the coming year."[6] This so-called "Period of Individual Solicitation" was to last for five years as money raising became a major task for the Executive Board and central staff alike. As sales of supplies and literature grew, these became a more reliable source of revenue. On October 31, 1911 a registration plan went into effect, and Scoutmasters and Commissioners were required to renew annually for a fee of 25 cents. Individual Scout registration did not go into effect until October 1913 with a fee of 25 cents per enrolled Scout, and then Scoutmasters were no longer charged. "The members of the National Council believe that every Scout will take more interest in this work if he is officially enrolled and has his name listed at the National office. They also realize that it is important to have a complete list of active Scouts available so that it will be possible to tell just how many Scouts there are in the country and where they are located."[7] Initially, a Scoutmaster had simply told headquarters how many Scouts he had. Membership figures were unreliable. Some estimates gave 300,000 as the 1911 Scout population but West believed that the original number was closer to 20,000 although 61,000 would later become the official 1911 enrollment.[8]

Badges, Awards and Insignia

Insignia and uniform became sources of conflict. Baden-Powell had first presented a fleur-de-lis badge to his South African Constabulary Scouts and modified it slightly for his Boy Scouts. The fleur-de-lis, lily, trefoil, or Scout arrowhead as the shape of the badge was variously called, was the basis for essentially all scout badges around the world; however, there were some, particularly Andrew Carnegie and the Peace Society, who thought that arrowheads signified war and were therefore too militaristic for boys. Baden-Powell wrote to West on April 5, 1911, "As is well known the origin of the trefoil, lily or shamrock as a badge is practically identical with that of the cross the fleur-de-lys or lily being practically used as the sign for purity. The trefoil badge of the Scouts is now used, with slight local variations, in almost every civilised country as the mark of our brotherhood for good citizenship and friendliness. I think it would be a great pity for the American Scouts to change from the Badge which is now universally recognized as that of our brother-hood."[9]

West agreed with Baden-Powell and this argument won. Beard then designed a badge with an American eagle superimposed on the trefoil. He insisted that the trefoil was really the North point of the compass and "has become an international emblem and is so recognized, and since I had the American eagle placed upon it for our Scouts, against the strenuous objections of some of our alien friends, I have withdrawn my objection to it."[10] Beard's eagle also prevailed over "our alien friend" Seton's suggested wolf as the symbol of the highest rank in Scouting. The British had only three ranks, Tenderfoot, Second Class, and First Class. The Americans modified these requirements (for example to explain the composition of the "National flag" rather than the Union Jack and to earn and deposit one dollar instead of sixpence.) They added Life, Star, and Eagle ranks for earning merit badges beyond First Class. A Life Scout had to earn merit badges in first aid, athletics, life saving, personal health and public health, a Star Scout five more, and an Eagle Scout any twenty-one. No specific merit badges were required to earn the Eagle badge until 1915.

Beard also prevailed with regard to the uniform. The South African Constabulary uniform consisted of a "short-sleeve khaki shirt, green tie, flat, wide-brimmed hat, shorts dismounted and breeches mounted, and rucksack on back."[11] For his Boy Scouts, Baden-Powell substituted a scarf for the tie (after Burnham) and a wooden stave for a gun. Beard argued that the American landscape was too rough for bare knees. Breeches, leggings, a high collar jacket, and high-peaked, broad-brimmed hat won out as the American uniform. It had a decidedly military look. West wanted to control the manufacture and distribution of uniforms and insignia not only for quality control, but also to prevent unauthorized use.[12] Initially, the Committee on Equipment produced just buttons but they soon made a complete uniform for a total cost of $ 2.15.

Troops of the South African Constabulary had been divided into "patrols" of six men under the supervision of a senior constable. Baden-Powell retained this structure for Boy Scouts as the Scoutmaster selected his Patrol Leaders. One argument that Beard lost was what to call a "Scoutmaster." His position was that the British had schoolmasters but Americans had schoolteachers and Americans would "bow to no master." His choice of a name for the troop leader is not recorded as he did not prevail.[13]

According to Levy, these symbols and insignia, the badges, uniform, Oath, Law, Motto, and slogan "not only fill an essential part of the incentive and ritual of membership, they serve an important function in maintaining good relations between the movement and the public - and intentionally so."[14] Scouting had a public face and the movement had a reputation to maintain. West would return to the need for proper uniform and insignia worn in the context of public service in order to retain that reputation, time and time again.

Organization and Supervision

From the very beginning, the principle of community organizations sponsoring troops under their own volunteer leaders prevailed. This was Scouting as a "movement." "The scheme is available as a movement to supplement the work of existing organizations rather than as an agency which might lessen the influence of existing organizations."[15] "The opportunity is afforded these organizations to introduce into their programs unique features appealing to interests which are universal among boys. The method is summed up under the term 'Scoutcraft,' and is a combination of observation, deduction, handiness or ability to do things. Scoutcraft includes first aid, life saving, tracking, signaling, nature study, seamanship, campcraft, woodcraft, chivalry, patriotism, and other subjects."[16]

As the organization grew, it was soon obvious that it was too large and too far-flung to be administered efficiently from New York City. "How to organize a local committee" was one of the first publications. A group of citizens led by a "Commissioner" (following the British designation of one who received a "commission" from Headquarters) formed a Local Council to supervise and provide support to troops within it. The Commissioner's role was to support the Scoutmaster. Scoutmasters might "need direction and want to feel that there is some one in the community who knows Scoutcraft better than they, to whom they can go for advice and help."[17] The Commissioner also convened the Council Court of Honor. "The Scout Court of Honor is the vehicle through which the local community gives articulate approval to scouts who have made progress. It exists primarily to encourage and stimulate, to standardize and interpret, to recognize and reward the boys' effort to advance and make progress through the scout ranks and tests."[18]

Some local councils paid their commissioners and some did not. So that they could maintain close contact with each troop, local councils were initially limited to a single county. Councils with a volunteer Commissioner were called Second Class Councils, and those with a paid Commissioner or Executive were called First Class Councils. First Class Councils got to keep fifteen cents of each quarter registration fee collected, but Second Class Councils could keep only five cents.

After all four organizing commissions had reported, the new Handbook was developed and five thousand copies printed in proof form. West later described the process. "There was also another remarkable experience we had with this book. There was such great anxiety on the part of those who were waiting for it that I had to ask Doubleday Page & Co., the publishers, to do something which they said they had never done before and they actually turned over to me the key to their plant. They said they couldn't get it out when I asked them to, but that if I could, I should go ahead. I organized a group of men who worked with me at night, supplementing the group that worked there in the day. I organized a secretarial staff and transferred my office to Garden City, and eleven days from the time I gave them the manuscript I had my 5000 books in complete form."[19] The handbooks were mailed to boys' workers as well as Scout leaders throughout the country for comments and suggestions. This helped consolidate support for the Scout movement as many men felt that they had input into the program.

While the commissions were hard at work, the Boy Scouts of America held its first annual meeting at the White House on February 8, 1911. West had asked President Taft to serve as Honorary President and to welcome the new Movement. Unfortunately, Taft had read none of the material West had prepared for him, and he would not have known why his visitors were there. With the approval of Taft's secretary, Mr. Norton, board member Lee Hammer breeched White House protocol and approached the President to thank him for inviting the group to explain to him what Scouting was all about, and Hammer then proceeded to do so. Taft graciously acknowledged the fine ideals of Scouting, and a public relations disaster was avoided.[20] Taft later said, "Boys, you and I are members of the same great organization and I am very proud of my membership. It is the great underlying purpose of the Boy Scouts of America organization that boys be trained to help others."[21] Each president since Taft has served as Honorary President of the BSA.

Taking Charge

West had been hired as "Managing Secretary" but soon upgraded his title and began signing himself as "Executive Secretary." On November 28, 1911 the Executive Board approved a change in title to "Chief Scout Executive." Beard was very unhappy about this and, for the next thirty years, complained about it to anyone who would listen. His letter to Treasurer Pratt is typical, "I don't know where he got the title, but it seems to have offended everyone, because he is not a Scout in the sense that they are, and hence, has not the ability to be the Chief Scout; he is essentially a secretary and a good one."[22] Despite Beard's objection, the title was consistent with the designations of Chief Scout (Seton), Chief Scout Citizen (Theodore Roosevelt), and Chief Scout Woodsman (Gifford Pinchot, head of the U. S. Forest Service). The titles of Chief Scout Surgeon, Stalker, Campmaster, and Directors of Health, Athletics, and Chivalry were created, but the positions were apparently never filled. Along with Bomus and Verbeck, Beard was one of three National Scout Commissioners. There was no Chief Scout Commissioner.

West's initial six-month commitment period passed seemingly unnoticed. On June 13 the Board raised his salary from four thousand dollars per year to five thousand retroactive to February 1 and to six thousand beginning July 1.[23] To put this salary in perspective, the Economic History Services website (*www.eh.net*) offers calculations based on multiple indices. Using the Consumer Price Index or relative purchasing power of a 1911 salary in 2005 dollars, a $5,000 salary in 1911 would be equivalent to a $106,000 salary in 2005. West was reasonably well paid.

"Mrs. West and the boy" finally moved from Washington to Forest Hills on Long Island and the family was reunited. West apparently did not spend much time with them. According to Julian Solomon:

> At work he drove himself with almost inexhaustible energy. In the early years he would arrive at the office at 8 AM and seldom leave before 5:30 or 6:00. The same hours were held on Saturdays, when a special personal stenographer and office boy were on duty for his sole assistance. When a special project was underway or there was a crisis to be met he would work until midnight or

beyond. He thought nothing of putting in 18 hour days when pressure was intense and he expected every other employee to do the same. In his excessive devotion to work there seemed to be a lack of compassion for other people.[24]

Salomon was one of those Scout office boys. On several occasions he and a secretary left on a train with West after dinner. West dictated letters and messages and the other two got off the train at the next stop and returned to Manhattan to mail them. On one occasion, West continued on to Buffalo and Salomon and the secretary got home from Albany at 3 AM. Salomon's father complained to West, but the practice continued.

> Every afternoon he [West] would leave his desk for a tour of the office, stopping at the desks of executives, secretaries, clerks, and office boys. He would question them about the day's work and suggest ways of doing it. He might stop to straighten a picture or neatly arrange a stack of papers or books on a shelf or desk. As inspector-general of the office boys, he would have them lined up, seeing to it that every detail of their [Scout] uniforms and the placement of their badges conformed exactly with the regulations in the *Handbook*. In his own dress he was a stickler for uniformity. His uniform in the early years was always the lawyer's frock coat and striped pants.[25]

West identified closely with the businessmen who dominated his board. He saw himself as the chief operating officer of a large institution and he wanted the perks of that office, such as a house, a club, and an expense account. While remaining deeply committed to a progressive social agenda, he was equally committed to the capitalist system that had precipitated the need for it. He was particularly attuned to the need to promote, advertise, and market his product, the Boy Scouts of America, and to exercise quality control over it. He counted his success in units of service provided. In his frock coat and striped pants, West would have been comfortable in any boardroom in America.

In February 1912 Baden-Powell came to America to lecture for the second time. The tour had originally been arranged by a New York promoter named Lee Keedick who agreed to pay Baden-Powell $15,000 to speak about his military experiences in twenty cities in five weeks. The Executive Board decided that it would be much better for the Scouting program if the Boy Scouts of America were in charge of the tour. In the spirit of "Individual Solicitation," they took up a collection and George Pratt of Standard Oil, Mortimer Schiff of Kuehn and Loeb, and financier John Sherman Hoyt each gave $5,000 to buy out the contract. West went along with B-P on the tour and made up the schedule of events, gave suggestions about the content of the lectures, and added lantern slides. He arranged for Baden-Powell to meet Andrew Carnegie, President Taft, and Teddy Roosevelt. Baden-Powell complained that West demanded too much of him and noted that American Scouts needed more discipline and that the organization should have better communication with its membership. *Boys' Life* reported the visit a bit differently:

> The tour of James E. West, Chief Scout [sic] of the Boy Scouts of America, across the country in company of Sir Robert Baden-Powell, Chief Scout of the British Boy Scouts, gave West a splendid opportunity to become acquainted with the recognized leader of the scout movement and to absorb many of his plans and ideas for the development of the scout movement. The relationship between Sir Robert and Mr. West developed into warm friendship in the five weeks that they were together. The letters which Sir Robert has written to the leaders of the scout movement and to Mr. West himself show that he has the utmost admiration for the ability of Mr. West and the work that he is accomplishing for the boys of the country.[26]

One incident marred the grand tour. On March 9 Baden-Powell and West were hooted off the stage in Portland, Oregon by International Workers of the World members incensed by what they perceived to be B-P's antiunion comments in the first printing of the Handbook.[27] The offending lines about speaking badly of employers may have been left out in the second printing, but the union men knew the enemy when they saw him. The Scouts were also feared as uniformed strike-breakers as they had already done this in some communities.

West then corresponded with Samuel Gompers, President of the American Federation of Labor, because "the sons of the laboring men make up such a large population of American boys, it is essential that we exercise special care in our aims and activities to be of help to them and merit the support of their parents."[28] West pointed out that the American Federation of Labor was reading the British manual and "the unfortunate early edition of our own Handbook" and confusing the Boy Scouts of America with the American Boy Scouts. Gompers could promise only that his Executive Council would "thoroughly investigate the Boy Scout movement."[29]

In addition to revising the handbook, West tried to appease unions in other ways. When an Illinois Commissioner complained that "union labor conditions make it impossible" for a non-union Scout to shoe a live horse for the Blacksmithing merit badge, West would allow the Scout to neither violate union rules nor substitute shoeing an amputated hoof.[30] This response spoke as much to West's rigidity as to his desire not to offend labor.

A very real problem in appealing to union members or to any working man was the decidedly middle-class face of the Boy Scouts of America. Each year the BSA published a demographic profile of its scoutmasters. Most were identified as clergymen, teachers, or "mercantiles." The Second Annual Report indicated that of the first 1500 Scoutmasters, 956 were college graduates. Four hundred sixty three were clergymen, 184 schoolteachers or administrators, and only 105 were mechanics.

In addition to union antipathy, there were other parts of American society that did not welcome Scouting. There was a "Negro problem" and then there were the Catholics. On September 15, 1911, West wrote a letter to D. D. Moore of the *New Orleans Time Democrat* in reply to Moore's letter that stated: "we cannot keep the white boys of this section in an organization that admits negroes."

West replied:

> Now in regard to the negro, [sic] this has been a great problem, but we believe that it is being handled in a way

which will meet the objections that might naturally be
expected from people in Louisiana and other southern
states. In fact in some of the southern states a plan has
been worked out successfully. In the first place, the local
council, when organized properly and recognized by this
office, is asked to work out a suitable plan with reference
to all such problems. There would be no necessity
whatever of the New Orleans Boy Scouts admitting
negro boys into their ranks. The negro interests in the
Boy Scout movement could be handled in the same way
as you handle the public schools in the south, that is,
providing separate schools, teachers, and administration.
If this matter is put up to the New Orleans local council
in a fair and clear manner I feel confident that you will
be able to handle the situation.[31]

A similar suggestion had come from Judge Taylor of St. Louis in
a letter to West dated November 14, 1912. He suggested that Negro
troops be assigned letters instead of numbers, that Negro scoutmasters
be appointed, and that the Negro Scoutmasters' Association appoint one
representative to the Local Council. "Either the negros [sic] are entitled
to the benefit of the Scout Movement or the whole Scout Movement
means nothing."[32] West's solution at the time was to follow local custom
regarding segregation.

The early association of Scouting with the YMCA led the Catholic hierarchy to view the Scout program as a "feeder" to that most
Protestant of organizations. In May 1911, The Pilot, the newspaper of
the Diocese of Boston, said that Scouting was a scheme of proselytism
"through the medium of literary and athletic association and movement." Parish schools should develop their own youth programs, but
"in the meantime every Catholic father and mother will refrain from
supporting the Boy Scout movement, and insist that their boys have
no affiliation with it."[33]

West argued that Scouting was nonsectarian and could be adopted
by any religious organization. In 1913 the Catholic Church relented,
but established strict guidelines for Catholic boys involved in Scouting
such as those of John Cardinal Farley in New York: troops must be ex-
clusively Catholic, representative Catholics must sit on local boards, the
scoutmaster must be approved by Catholic authority, and no Catholic

boy may join the Scouts unless he is a member of the Junior Holy Name Society or some kindred religious sodality.[34]

Similarly, in March 1913 the Young Men's Mutual Improvement Association of the Latter-Day Saints voted to affiliate their Mutual Improvement Association Scouts with the Boy Scouts of America but to maintain exclusivity and their own program features and Commissioners. This immediately added 15,000 Scouts to the national BSA program.

Boys' Life

West did put one of B-P's suggestions into action. The Rhode Island Boy Scouts had published a magazine called *Boys' Life* since January 1912. On April 22, West wrote to Joseph Lane, the Editor in Providence: "Would you consider a proposition to purchase all of your equity outright and to employ yourself and possibly your advertising manager for $3,000 cash? Or $5,000 to be paid over five years from proceeds of the magazine, that is subscriptions and advertising with interest at the rate of 6% per annum, we having the right to pay off the entire amount earlier if desired?"[35] At this time *Boys' Life* claimed a paid circulation of 7,000 and newsstand sales of 30,000 for each issue.

On April 23 George Barton, the publisher, made a counteroffer of $8,000, with $5,000 in cash and three annual payments of $1,000 at 6% or $7,500 in cash. After negotiation, a final deal was announced on June 6 - $6,000 with $2,000 to be paid by November 1, $2,000 within twelve months, and $2,000 within eighteen months. Frank Presbrey of Presbrey Advertising and Chair of the BSA Editorial Committee made the first payment from his own funds. On July 1, 1912 the Scouts had a national magazine. Lane did not come along as Editor. Seton and Beard both contributed columns but Seton had some concerns. In a January 5, 1914 letter to West, Seton railed against the support of chewing gum:

> I protest against the *Boys' Life* or any other magazine that I can influence advertising or referring to the gum habit except to denounce it as a filthy, degrading practice, borrowed from the lowest negros [sic] of the cotton-field, and fastened upon our youth as a dope habit by the unscrupulous gum trust. I hope we shall soon have a gum ordinance, forbidding all Scouts the use of gum, even more stringently than the use of tobacco.[36]

Good Turns

Community good turns became an integral part of Scouting. In 1912 the Scouts had promoted a "Safe and Sane Fourth of July," and in 1913, 548 Scouts had provided services to veterans of both sides at the Fiftieth Anniversary of the Battle of Gettysburg. They assisted the Red Cross and helped veterans in many ways, such as rendering first aid, erecting tents, carrying water and food, and guiding the men. Scouts rendered similar service at both Confederate and Grand Army of the Republic reunions as long as they were held. Scouts assisted at floods in Ohio and Indiana by rescuing people and property, providing messenger service, and collecting food, clothing, and money for distribution by the Red Cross. Fifteen hundred Scouts provided crowd control and first aid in Washington, D.C. on March 3, 1913 for the Suffragette Parade and on March 4 for President Wilson's inauguration. Scouts tried to live up to West's vision of them:

> The real Boy Scout is not a 'sissy.' He is not a hothouse plant, like little Lord Fauntleroy. There is nothing 'milk and water' about him; he is not afraid of the dark. He does not do bad things because he is afraid of being decent. Instead of being a puny, dull, or bookish lad who dreams and does nothing, he is full of life, energy, enthusiasm, bubbling over with fun, full of ideas as to what he wants to do and he knows how he wants to do it. He has many ideals and many heroes. He is not hitched to his mother's apron strings. While he adores his mother and would do anything to save her from suffering or discomfort, he is self-reliant, sturdy, and full of vim. He is just the sort of boy his father is proud to own as his son.[37]

Service projects were publicized as evidence that Scouting was building character in boys. To this Beard wryly noted: "the Scouts are a fine lot of lads, but apparently, they were a fine lot of lads before they joined." This observation was later confirmed by a 1931 study by Fairchild who again concluded in "Conduct habits of Boy Scouts," that "the Scouts had fewer behavior problems than other boys because they had fewer behavior problems before they joined."[38] Despite this finding, the BSA has always promoted itself as a "character building" organization and press releases from the National Council have publicized public service activities since 1912.[39]

From the earliest days, West tried to promote Scouting as an educational endeavor, but he was also committed to the religious component. In response to a question from Robinson, "Do you regard it as desirable that the Movement should be more and more educational and less and less religious in character?" West answered, "Most decidedly I do not, nor do I know of anyone in authority who does."[40] On the other hand, he proudly pointed out in 1914 that "the postal authorities recognized the BSA as an 'institution of learning' and granted them privileges of second class mailing peculiar to such institutions."[41] West also thought that adult leaders should know how to teach. By 1914 Columbia and fifteen other colleges and universities were offering courses for Scoutmasters, and Culver Military Academy had begun a residential training program. For continuing education, *Scouting*, a magazine for adult leaders, was first published on April 15, 1913.

Militarism

A March 13, 1913 article in the *Washington Star* praised the use of the scout stave: "The work done by the Boy Scouts Monday in their effort to hold the crowd in check that the suffragists might march uncontested shows that the staff is the most important part of their equipment." The paper went on to point out that "boys in the uniform that stands for learning the principles of good citizenship [were] actually restraining grown men from acting the part of brutes."[42] Seton, on the other hand, had written to the Board on November 21, 1912, that terms like "troop" and "patrol" were inappropriate and that the use of the stave as a "dummy musket" was too militaristic.

West worked very hard to define Scouting as non-military. In a July 17, 1916 speech to the National Education Association convention, he defined military training as "military tactics and maneuvers of utility only to army life" and gave as examples "sham battles, manual of arms, sabre and bayonet drills, skirmish work, army engineering, and the study of army organizations." He pointed out that in Scout training, "those things which make for discipline, obedience, loyalty, courtesy, endurance, resourcefulness, initiative, alertness, moral courage, good health, knowledge of how to care for oneself, etc. should not be considered destructive military training but should be given as part of citizenship training to all boys and girls to properly prepare them primarily for their later responsibilities as home makers, wage earners, and citizens." He suggested that Scouting was, in fact, a movement for peace. "In thus making available to boys of all classes a common meeting ground where they may play and compete and learn to know that the other fellow is not much different from themselves, the Boy Scout Movement is performing a distinctive patriotic service and the observance of the scout law and the tremendous cumulative value of the required daily good turn, and the creation of better feeling among millions of scouts in our own and other lands constitute a latent but powerful and rapidly growing factor for universal good will and the brotherhood of man."[43]

The charge of militarism first arose in April 1912, when an American Boy Scout accidentally shot a little boy. West hastened to distance the Boy Scouts of America from Hearst's American Boy Scouts and the tragedy. "The Boy Scouts of America is entirely a peace movement, both in theory and practice in that it bans all military practices and that its program of activities is confined to wholesome achievements for the purpose of developing character."[44] When West referred to that American Boy Scout as an "imitation Scout", Beard fired off a letter to West objecting to "expression of contempt for a rival; this is undignified and does not accord with the strict interpretation of the moral code as we preach it to our boys."[45]

The 1911 handbook included a merit badge for Marksmanship. The single requirement was to "qualify as a marksman in accordance with the regulations of the National Rifle Association." Probably to appease Carnegie and the Peace Movement, however, the BSA awarded no badges in 1911 and only 12 in 1912. In 1913 Remington Arms became interested in developing a long range program of shooting as a sport, and they produced the Model 4S or American Boy Scout .22 caliber rifle. The American Boy Scouts embraced the gun immediately and sold it from their headquarters for five dollars. They did not sell the bayonet made to fit it. The Boy Scouts of America would not adopt it. Remington salesmen were encouraged to ask Scouts and Scoutmasters to write to national headquarters in order to request that the marksmanship badge be issued. Through Col. Bomus, the National Rifle Association also lobbied the Executive Board to issue the badge.[46]

Teddy Roosevelt weighed in on guns as well, refusing a request by New York City Scouts to appear at a rally at Madison Square Garden. He wrote: "A Boy Scout who is not trained actively and affirmatively that it is his duty to bear arms for the country in time of need is at least negatively trained to be a sissy; and there cannot be anything worse for this country than to have an organization of boys brought up to accept the mushy milk and water which is the stock in trade of the apostles of pacifism."[47] It probably did not help to calm his belligerence that his Scout membership card read: "The Boy Scout Plan - not military, teaching however, loyalty, patriotism, chivalry, advocating universal peace." Col. Leonard Wood resigned from the Executive Board because of a pacifist article in the November 1914 issue of *Boys' Life* by Andrew Carnegie that Wood deemed "almost treasonable." The article was accompanied by a poem entitled "When Some Fellow's Daddy Kills Some Fellow's Daddy." Roosevelt agreed with Wood that this issue of *Boys' Life* was unpatriotic. West clearly got the message. He restrained the antiwar rhetoric and awarded more Marksmanship merit badges (88 in 1915). He still would not sell guns, however.

West did redefine his position on militarism, noting:

> As an organization the Scout Movement is not military in thought, form, or spirit, although it does instill in boys the military virtues such as honor, loyalty, obedience, and patriotism. The uniform, the patrol, the troop, and the drill are not for military tactics; they are for the unity, the harmony and the rhythm of spirit that boys learn in Scouting. It is in the wearing of the uniform and doing of things together as Scouts that they absorb the force and truth of the Scout law which states: 'A Scout is a friend to all, and a brother to every other Scout.'[48]

The most obvious victim of the escalating militancy and American jingoism was Ernest Thompson Seton and the primary stone-thrower was Daniel Carter Beard. Beard's primary motivation in attacking Seton was to be recognized as the founder of Scouting and to eliminate Seton as a rival for that honor.

The argument began in 1910. In a letter to Beard, Seton proposed that priority in recognition as founder should be based on the date of publication of the first mention of a boys' program. Seton's first article had appeared in May 1902, Beard's in September 1905, and Baden-Powell's in August 1906. "Baden-Powell however is responsible for three important things which have made the movement a worldwide success. First, the official use of the name 'Boy Scouts;' second the element of thrift; third the element of altruism. Everyone who knows the facts knows that my movement was practically identical with that of Baden-Powell so that I do not see how you coming three years later should claim priority over me as well as Baden-Powell." Beard made a marginal note: "This is beating around the bush. Seton knows that my Society of Scouts was the original one and that he called upon me and got the scheme by cross questioning me on the subject."[49] He really appeared to believe this.

In a September 14, 1910 speech, Baden-Powell had called all three of them "Uncles of the Movement." This appeased no one. In a letter to naturalist William Hornaday, Seton wrote, "I think perhaps the fairest summing up of the whole situation is this: Beard, Baden-Powell and myself all set out to do exactly the same thing. I was the first to give the public the definite thought. Baden-Powell was last, but he did it best. He has not been very fair in his treatment of others; but what does it matter? We should think, rather, of the boys we are trying to help, and not worry over who was the one that brought the message."[50] Robinson pointed out that the key point in Seton's argument was an ambiguous phrase in a January 24, 1908 letter from Baden-Powell to Seton, "We are going on with my scheme like your Woodcraft Indians." B-P emphasized the "my" and Seton the "like."[51]

George Pratt, the BSA Treasurer, cautioned Beard, "I have noticed in some of the magazines that you are still speaking about who was the originator of the Boy Scouts. You surely realize that this is going to make friction when Seton returns, and I ask you, for the good of the movement, to please discontinue making any reference to who discovered it."[52] Beard ignored him.

Beard used a different argument with West with regard to Seton, "I shall always claim that mine was and is a boy scout society, the first one organized. His had for its ideals a lot of bloody savages, mine a splendid lot of manly white men of the best type of American manhood."[53] In 1913 he wrote: "We have for our Chief Scout, a very distinguished subject of Great Britain, an alien who has stated in unequivocal language his disapproval of the principles upon which this country was founded, and made disparaging remarks about our flag."[54]

Seton had tried to clarify his position in a letter to Beard:

> As to the references to the flag, I never in my life said or thought such things as you ascribe to me. I remember perfectly well the occasion you probably have in mind. We were good naturedly discussing the [Campfire] Club [of America] flag at the Governors' meeting. I said, 'Do let's have something artistic. The only national flag that has any art merit is the Japanese.' Someone said, 'What's the matter with the Stars and Stripes?' I replied, 'It's as bad as the British flag and that's pretty bad.' Any more than this has been added by others.

In his marginal note, Beard wrote, "His memory is greatly at fault. He denounced our country as the 'rottenest one on earth' our flag as the ugliest and our article on patriotism as false but he used a stronger term."[55]

In 1915 Seton again appealed to Beard:

> Four years ago you gave me your word of honor that you would not again put forth the claim to being the Founder of the Boy Scouts . . . You can say what you think among your private friends, but the fair and honorable thing for you now is to make no public claim to any such distinction, but let the matter be settled by the slow, sure process of history. In the interest of harmony I appeal to your manly sense of fair play to drop the unprofitable discussion together with everything that might tend to revive it.[56]

Beard responded:

> O come off, Seton; don't make a fool of yourself. Not interested in the dates. Have no knowledge of the

articles to which you refer. Have neither power nor
desire to muzzle press. You make me tired. Not guilty!
If you really want to fight would suggest that you will
be welcomed in the trenches as 'ENGLAND EXPECTS
ALL LOYAL SONS TO DO THEIR DUTY!' Please let
this close the incident.[57]

Executive Board President Livingstone weighed in and wrote
West: "It should be the fundamental policy at headquarters that everyone contributing ideas, helpful or otherwise, should receive due
credit for them, and the credit should persist in as far as is practical."[58]
Robinson summarized the dilemma as "B-P could not help thinking
in military terms; Seton could not help thinking in terms of the Ideal
Indians; Beard thought in terms of the 'Knights of Buckskin' or the old
time frontiersmen who conquered the forest and killed the Indians."[59]
It was left to West to resolve the conflict.

West's solution to the conflicting claims was to reinforce a direct
link from Baden-Powell through William Boyce to the incorporation of
the BSA, and to bypass both Seton and Beard. This version of history
included the fabrication of Boyce's meeting with B-P and the trunk of
materials. The fog is another part of the story. A history of the Rhode
Island Boy Scouts points out that in 1911, Captain George Bucklin was
lost in the fog in Providence and a Rhode Island Boy Scout refused a
tip for showing him to his destination. Bucklin was so impressed by this
good turn that he left the Scouts an endowment in his will.[60] Helping
businessmen lost in a city fog is either an archetypal Scouting activity
or a better story than helping them cross the street in front of a hotel.
The original story may have persisted as the proverbial good deed of a
Scout's helping a little old lady across the street - better a little old lady
than a hesitant businessman. Bill Hillcourt reported that he had reviewed
the weather reports in the *London Times* for the period that Boyce was
in England, and there was no fog at that time.[61] The Unknown Scout
did do two important things: he impressed Boyce and he gave West a
way to downplay the roles of Seton and Beard.

As Chief Scout, Seton had no role in Scouting except as a columnist
in *Boys' Life*, but he was still an immensely popular figure. West was
reluctant to lose his support; however, Seton was not reelected Chief

Scout at the Annual Meeting in February 1915. His name was still on the National BSA letterhead and this caused Beard to complain about "an alien's name ahead of the advocate of Americanism." Seton's last column appeared in the May 15 issue of *Boys' Life* and his name was dropped from the magazine's masthead on August 15. West had many suggestions ranging from Roosevelt's "leaders should be citizens" to John Alexander's "let him resign or give him something to do." It was hard for West to come down on the issue of citizenship because Robinson, a Canadian, and Alexander, a Scot, were still members of the Executive Board and not U.S. citizens either.

Finally, Seton himself broke the impasse and took the battle to the pages of the *New York Times*. Under the December 6, 1915 headline "Seton Still Insists on Quitting Scouts - Puts the Blame on West" Seton summed up the history of Scouting as "Seton started it; Baden-Powell boomed it; West killed it." He went on to say, "It should be clearly stated, and I want it understood, that I esteem the Executive Board of the Boy Scouts to be a splendid lot of men, giving freely of their time and money to the work. My only criticism is that they have allowed all direction and power to centre in the hands of James E. West, a lawyer, who is a man of great executive ability but without knowledge of the activities of boys, who has no point of contact with boys, and who, I might almost say, has never seen the blue sky in his life." Seton insisted that he had resigned in order to devote more time to the Woodcraft League. He has not taken out American citizenship, he said, because he did not want to appear to be deserting England when she was at war.[62]

West responded the next day in the New York Times article titled: "West Says Seton is not a Patriot—Is in Harmony with Anarchists' Views."

> When it was discovered that Mr. Seton was in harmony with the views of anarchists on the question as to whether the Boy Scouts of America should stand for patriotism and good citizenship, no time was lost in developing the issue . . . [He] contended that the Boy Scouts of America should not undertake to have boys pledge allegiance to their country, but should leave them free to support our country when they thought our country was right and to damn it when they thought it

was wrong. He personally made clear that he damned
our country for most of its past history. This is the real
and only reason that Mr. Seton is not now Chief Scout
of the Boy Scouts of America.[63]

A milder version of West's response appeared in the January 1916
issue of *Boys' Life* under the heading "Why Mr. Seton is Not Chief
Scout."

Mr. Seton was dropped because he was not a citizen
of the United States and refused to say that he would
become one, and because he was not in sympathy with
American customs and ideals.

The Scout Movement is in no wise affected by the
dropping of Mr. Seton. The program, followed since
1910, is not dependent upon any individual. Mr. Seton
was not a member of the Editorial Board which compiled
the original handbook and contributed nothing to the
preparation of the first chapter which completely covers
the scout program and the scheme of organization. The
comparatively small number of pages of material written
by Mr. Seton are interesting, but nothing essential to
the program of Scouting. They can be easily replaced in
future editions by eminent American citizens.[64]

This sentiment was considerably different from that which West
had written in the Second Annual Report only three years earlier: "The
organization will ever be under obligation to Mr. Seton for his unremit-
ting zeal and effort to produce this book and for his willingness to send
it out in an uncompleted form in order to meet the insistent requests
from the field."[65]

Robinson had a different perspective on Seton's conflict:

The English Movement had in its Chief Scout, Baden-
Powell an embodiment of its ideal. The American
Movement had no such man to embody its ideals.
Seton was chosen as Chief Scout but he embodied the
Woodcraft Indians ideals more than he did those

of the Boy Scouts. B-P though listening to advice from every quarter, dominated his Movement. Seton wanted to dominate the American Movement as Chief Scout, but could not. At the beginning he gave himself wholeheartedly to the Movement and for a while was its greatest asset. Gradually it dawned upon him that this new American Movement was not merely an adaptation of his unique program, but something different   something that welcomed certain ideas from his program, but refused to accept all. Because it strongly favored B-P's program rather than his, a tinge of jealousy crept in and some bitterness. He felt that he had freely given much to B-P's program, but that B-P had contributed nothing to his own program.

Mr. West, as Executive Secretary, came between Seton and the Executive Board in the sense that his views generally prevailed rather than those of Mr. Seton. After several years of increasing dissatisfaction, Seton resigned, - an embittered and heartbroken man.[66]

West also had a personal score to settle. At some point Seton had invited West and others to his home in Cos Cob, Connecticut. In what was an obvious attempt to embarrass West, he handed him a fire by friction set and gave him the "honor" of lighting the fire. As West later recounted to Irving Crump, he had read and observed, and was good with his hands. He got the spark, blew up the flame, and lit the fire "to his own delight and satisfaction" and to Seton's chagrin.[67]

Seton was gone. The 1916 revision of the handbook removed the last vestiges of his material. Beard was left, however, and he continued to press for recognition as the true founder of American Scouting. West would have to deal with this issue for another quarter century.

Notes

[1] Helen West, personal communication
[2] Baden-Powell, R. S. S. "How the Scouts' badge originated." *Boys' Life* 7/28 page 18
[3] Quoted by Murray, William. *History of the Boy Scouts of America.* New York: BSA, 1937, page 54
[4] *Scouting* 10/20, page 16
[5] Baden-Powell, page 18
[6] Murray, page 66
[7] *Boys' Life* 10/14 page 22
[8] West, James E. "Historic statement of the Boy Scouts of America." Mimeo 1/1/30 page 11
[9] Baden-Powell letter in BSA Archives
[10] Beard, D.C. LOC 209 12/18/14 (Unless otherwise noted, "LOC" refers to the file box number in the Beard Archives at the Library of Congress.)
[11] Baden-Powell, R.S.S. "Where the Boy Scouts partly started." *Boys' Life* 4/28 page58
[12] Second Annual Report of the BSA page 13
[13] E.M. Robinson (EMR) Archives at Springfield College
[14] Levy, Harold. *Building a Popular Movement.* New York: Russell Sage Foundation, 1944 page 30
[15] *Scouting* 5/16 page 5
[16] *Boys' Life* 7/12 page 17
[17] Second Annual Report page 9
[18] *Community Boy Leadership.* BSA. 1921 page 213
[19] West, Historic Statement page 10
[20] Ibid
[21] *Scouting* 5/17 page 21
[22] Beard LOC 98 1/22/13
[23] Beard LOC 128 minutes of 6/13/11
[24] Salomon, J. *Three Great Scouts and a Lady.* Unpublished manuscript 1976 page 123a
[25] Salomon page 123b
[26] *Boys' Life* 6/12 page 17
[27] *New York Times* 3/10/12 page 1
[28] 9/29/11 letter in Theodore Roosevelt Archives LOC
[29] 12/15/11 letter in Theodore Roosevelt Archives LOC
[30] Beard LOC 128 5/17/12
[31] Beard LOC 128 4/22/12
[32] Ibid
[33] Quoted in *Boston Post* 5/01/11

[34] Roman Catholic Bulletin 11-17. "Suggestions regarding the formation of Roman Catholic troops."

[35] Beard LOC 128 4/22/12

[36] Beard LOC 129 1/05/14

[37] West, J. E. "The real Boy Scout" in *Leslie's Weekly* 4/18/12 page 448

[38] Quoted by Levy, page 88

[39] Second Annual Report page 118

[40] *Scouting* 5/15/16 page 5

[41] Fourth Annual Report page 13

[42] Beard LOC 128 3/13/13

[43] Copy in West file, Springfield College Library

[44] Third Annual Report page 35

[45] Beard LOC 128 4/24/12

[46] Grant, J. *Boys' Book of Single Shot Rifles.* New York: Wm. Morrow & Co. 1967

[47] Beard LOC 129 11/30/15

[48] Fourth Annual Report page 5

[49] Beard LOC 209 9/14/10

[50] Beard LOC 14 12/19/11

[51] EMR Archives

[52] Beard LOC 98 3/10/11

[53] Beard LOC 128 8/11

[54] Beard LOC 128 4/10/13

[55] Beard LOC 110 5/22/12

[56] Beard LOC 110 11/26/15

[57] EMR Archives 11/13/15 Although Beard appeared to save everything, this letter is not in the Library of Congress!

[58] Beard LOC 209 undated

[59] EMR Archives 1948

[60] Williams, J. H. *Scout Trail 1910-1962.* Providence, RI: Narragansett Council, BSA 1964

[61] Hillcourt, William, personal communication

[62] *New York Times* 12/06/15

[63] *New York Times* 12/07/15

[64] *Boys' Life* 1/16 page 28

[65] Second Annual Report page 5

[66] EMR Archives 1948 page 10

[67] Crump, I. "Thirty years of service to others" in *Boys' Life* 1/41 page 16

Chapter 4

The Great Wars

The second half of Scouting's first decade was characterized by a series of Great Wars. The enemies included Germany, The American (now United States) Boy Scouts, pulp fiction, and the Girl Scouts. Another war, "dreamers vs. bureaucrats," had already been going on for years and would continue for more than two decades. James E. West was the commanding general in all the battles.

Dreamers vs. Bureaucrats

After Seton left the organization, the only person that stood between Dan Beard and recognition as the "Founder" was, in Beard's opinion, James E. West. "Dreamers vs. bureaucrats" was a Beard phrase. His position is well-summarized in a June 12, 1916 letter which Beard wrote but did not send to West:

> Our Chief Scout's disloyalty was known to you from the start, but no action was taken upon it until such time as you found that the Chief Scout was in your way, the same is tru [sic] of my late Chief of staff and the same would be true of me if I should be in the way of your personal ambition. We might as well be frank about this thing, you know it and I know it, and you know that I know it, but my dear Mr. West this policy of yours will not win in the end, you may make it so disagreeable for me that I will be forced to leave the organization, but I want to point out to you that I am

> one of the last of the original dreamers, men of artistic
> and literary education from whose souls are involved
> [sic] the big ideas which other men organize and carry
> out to successful issues and when the last of us is driven
> from the movement by a series of presecutions [sic] then
> the movement itself will have lost its soul and become
> a machine composed of dictagraphs and card indexes,
> a dead machine which only runs from the momentum
> of the original impulse.[1]

Beard was not as shy in making his opinion known on other occasions, however. With regard to the chapter on signaling in the new 1915 handbook, he wrote: "It is absolutely hopeless to expect a betterment of the present situation as long as those whose duties are executive insist in passing on matters with which they are totally unfamiliar and on which they cannot be expected to be informed."[2] Similarly, when Seton's new Woodcraft manual was published, Beard wrote to West: "It has a oneness and a personal character which is sadly wanting in our composite production, besides which it is full of picturesque items which appeal to boys and children, but which have no meaning or weight with business and executive minds."[3] Beard could stand neither bureaucrats nor writing by committee.

Beard kept up a lively correspondence with some members of the Executive Board. To Frank Presbrey he wrote:

> Now, the executive has never put one original idea in
> the organization. He has never done one single thing
> that interest [sic] the boys themselves. As a boy's man,
> he is an absolute failure. He has not their sympathy or
> affection. That is his misfortune, not his fault, he was
> never a boy himself, but out of the original popularity
> of the Scout movement he has built up a wonderful
> organization, he has made himself a power in the land,
> he is an astute politician and accomplished diplomat,
> but a movement of this kind needs something else.[4]

After a complaint about where Beard was seated at a luncheon and how he had been introduced, West once wrote, "The responsibilities

. . . are such as to justify me in asking your help in every way in your power, that I might give the maximum time to these important matters. I sincerely hope that you will overlook anything which might appear as a slight, as I assure you that such a thing is not our desire or intention. It will help very much if you will assume this attitude."[5] Beard did not. West even showed a rare flash of humor in responding to one missive, " My Dear Commissioner Beard, I appreciated very much your characteristic letter of September 12th. Sincerely and cordially yours."[6]

When Beard accused West of the "crime of disloyalty" by publishing the English *Wolf Cubs Handbook*, West responded, "Personally, I do very much resent as unkind and unjust a suggestion of unAmericanism in any degree on the part of myself or others in our officer [sic] here in handling the matter." Beard wrote in the margin, "Ignore it."[7]

All of this must have been particularly annoying to West because Beard wrote at a desk and on a typewriter that West had authorized the organization to provide him in 1914. West apparently tolerated Beard because of the message Boyce had brought back from England: the Boy Scouts of America need an American icon. Beard fit that image; however, the man in buckskins sniped at the structure of the organization for the rest of his long life. Helen West suggested that her father actually enjoyed the verbal and written duels with Beard because of the intellectual challenge that they presented. They also reinforced West's perception of his need to retain control over his icon.

United States Boy Scouts

The Great War over names continued as West would not tolerate another organization identifying itself as "Scout." Commercialization of the "Scout" name was equally repugnant to him. Conflicts with other "Boy Scout" organizations were finally resolved in 1919, but West never satisfactorily brought a conclusion to the "Girl Scout problem."

On June 15, 1916 the Boy Scouts of America was formally chartered by Congress, and joined the American Red Cross as the only organizations so recognized. (The American Legion was third in 1919.) The legislation was rushed through with many other bills on a late night, voice vote as Congress rushed to adjourn for the Democratic convention; however, the fact remained that it passed. This chartered status would serve as the basis for further legal action against rival groups. It also required American citizenship of leaders and eliminated "alien" Scoutmasters.

William Randolph Hearst's American Boy Scouts had essentially died out in 1913 after the bad publicity as a result of the shooting and an isolationist, anti-military feeling in the country. In 1915 they arose from the ashes as the United States Boy Scouts (USBS). These boy scouts carried rifles and solicited war funds. John Gluck, a professional charity solicitor who kept 40% of what he raised, was the force behind the rival group. His Scouts were frequently confused with the Boy Scouts of America and West wanted to eliminate the confusion. Although the USBS claimed a membership of five thousand boys, only two hundred and fifty of these lived outside the state of New York. Consequently, the BSA filed suit against the USBS in the New York State Supreme Court on July 30, 1917. Charles Evans Hughes, prominent New York City attorney, former Governor of New York, and future Chief Justice of the United States Supreme Court, represented the BSA. On January 19, 1918 the USBS offered to settle for $8,000. The BSA refused. On March 11 the Court found for the BSA. The USBS settled without cost but the "prayer of relief" was granted, and they could not use the terms "Boy Scout," "Scout," or "Scouting." Gluck's organization persisted as the American Cadets for a few years, but it was never again a threat to the BSA. The battles against commercialization of the "Scout" name persisted for years, and it would be another decade before West could finally declare victory in that war.

Girl Scouts

The Girl Scouts were a different story. When Baden-Powell held his first Scout Rally at the Crystal Palace in 1909, he was chagrined to find girls wearing uniforms, carrying staves, and trying to participate. He refused to let them join his organization, but he did acknowledge the need for a program for girls. He encouraged his sister Agnes (and later his wife, Olave) to organize what he called "Girl Guides" and he helped write the manual. After Juliette Gordon Low followed B-P's model and organized a Girl Guide Group in Savannah, Georgia in 1912, she was persuaded by the girls themselves to change the name from Girl Guides to "Girl Scouts" to "ride right along on the wave with the Boy Scouts."[8] West said, "When Girl Scout troops were developed which were for all intents and purposes Boy Scout troops in activity and in conduct, this caused us a real heartache."[9] On February 18, 1918 West met with Girl Scout leaders. He later said that his position was that outdoor activity could be encouraged, but he stressed the fact that "girls should be brought up so as to be willing to be home makers."[10]

West frequently pointed out that Camp Fire Girls were home-oriented and therefore had advantages over the Girl Scouts. He did not point out that he had helped Luther Gulick organize the Camp Fire Girls in 1911. Although West was not a formal member of the "Committee on the Organization of an Association for Girls that shall Correspond to the Boy Scouts for Boys," the first press release about the Camp Fire Girls was issued from the National Headquarters of the BSA on April 10, 1911.

> Plans now are being made for a temporary organization called 'The Camp Fire Girls of America' which may develop into a national society in the fall if such a step seems justified. The aim of the organization is to provide for girls outdoor activities corresponding to those furnished boys by the Boy Scout movement. It seeks to encourage a greater interest among girls in exercises in the open with the threefold aim of developing their bodies, mind and characters. It is recognized, however, that the activities provided for the girls must be fundamentally different from those of boys and that special attention must be paid to the home.[11]

On March 11 Gulick told his Organizing Committee: "To copy the Boy Scout movement would be utterly and fundamentally evil, and would probably produce ultimately a moral and psychological involution which is the last thing in the world that any of us want. We hate manly women and womanly men, but we all do love to have a woman who is thoroughly womanly."[12] He later wrote:

> The Boy Scouts of America created a tangible possibility of the success of this work, but has in no sense served as a model for its organization. Feminine activity must have a kind of romance not necessary to the boy. In

> planning the work with the girl definitely in mind, the
> home and the community, which is the larger home,
> was made the center about which the movement was
> builded [sic]. The symbol is fire; lacking fire a home is a
> cheerless institution. Fire is symbolic of home, friends,
> and comfort. In introducing the camp theme the idea
> was not to compel girls to live in tents but to bring the
> simplicity of the out-of-door spirit into daily life. By
> making feminine activity attractive, girls are taught to
> like domestic things. By these means girls are shown the
> romance and the beauty of feminine work.[13]

These were West's sentiments exactly.

West argued that "I personally have endeavored to give leadership as best I know how, to show to all interested in girls' work that we who were in boys' work believe there is just as much need for aggressive, intelligent leadership in providing a program for girls, as there is in promoting one for boys."[14] Just don't call them Girl Scouts. West stressed that his men in the field told him that boys did not want to be Scouts if girls were Scouts, but "there has grown up among the Girl Scout people a notion that the only person in the United States who is opposed to the Girl Scouts is James E. West, and that he is inspiring an active propaganda in opposition to the Girl Scouts, which greatly handicaps me in my administrative responsibilities."[15] He didn't say it wasn't true. On May 16, 1918 the Girl Scouts formally notified West that they would not give up their name.[16] In 1919 West asked Baden-Powell to intercede with Mrs. Low because of his relationship with her. Baden-Powell said he would, but he never did. A bachelor of long standing, he was enroute to the United States with the widowed Mrs. Low when he fell in love with Olave Soames, a younger woman aboard the ship. He soon married her and rightly believed that he didn't have much influence with Juliette Low any longer. West continued to be at odds with the Girl Scouts for his entire tenure as Chief Scout Executive.

Pulp Fiction

As far as West was concerned, he had better luck in his Great War against words. Reading had given him his first opportunities for success and reading programs were his passion. When Franklin K. Mathiews walked into Scout Headquarters in 1912, it could have been by divine inspiration. Mathiews was a Baptist minister and scoutmaster with a mission. West subscribed to that mission wholeheartedly. The fact that Mathiews had gone to school with one of the Rockefellers probably didn't hurt either. As Mathiews later defined the Reading Program, its purpose was to strengthen character building and citizenship through the printed page. The Scouts would publish wholesome stories, recommend good books, and "keep off the bookstand and out of the market, reading matter which has a pernicious influence on the lives of boys."[17] Mathiews called himself the "Consulting Book Physician." In magazines such as *Ladies' Home Journal, Woman's Home Companion*, and *Delineator* as well as in Scout publications, Mathiews announced, "if parents would send to the National Headquarters of the Boy Scouts of America descriptions of their boys - age, interests, temperament, attainments, moral qualifications, faults or delinquencies - giving some idea of how the boys are inclined to spend their leisure time and the characteristics of the boys with whom they like best to associate, after careful examination of this statement, a course of reading would be prescribed which, it was believed, would not only interest the boys, but also help the parents in securing such results as would count for character-culture." He claimed to have received "hundreds of replies."[18]

The Board chose to be consistent with titles and named Mathiews "Chief Scout Librarian." Mathiews referred to himself as "Chief Scout Bookworm" in the December 1912 issue of *Boys' Life*, but he only used that title once. He was given a desk and paid for a half day a week, but his mission could not be confined to Tuesday afternoons.

Mathiews hated pulp fiction. In a 1914 article in *The Outlook*, he railed against "mile-a-minute fiction" with improbable plots "blowing out the boy's brains."[19] "The boy is confronted with a grave peril; on the one hand, there may be presented to him stories too sensational either because of gross exaggeration or because of low standards of moralities, not to speak of immoralities; or, on the other hand, the heroes may be unworthy either because of their low ideals or because their life is not purposeful, not full of the right sort of ambition to make the most of themselves."[20] Mathiews was particularly upset about "Scout fiction." "Authors and publishers, greedy for gain, have been quick to see that at the moment the most compelling interest in the mind of the American boy today is the Boy Scout idea. So we now have, though our Movement was incorporated only four years ago, scores and scores of Boy Scout story books absolutely unworthy to bear that name, not only because our principles are so grossly misrepresented, but also because the ideals presented are of the most pernicious sort."[21] Boy Scouts were not helping the King, Kaiser, or Uhlan, nor performing heroic deeds on airships, submarines, or motorcycles as some contemporary titles suggested.

Mathiews' solution was to publish something different. "Give him [the boy] the stories in which the heroes have the characteristics the boy so much admires - men of unquenchable courage, immense resourcefulness, absolute fidelity, conspicuous greatness; the men who do things, big things, wonderful things; the men who conquer and overcome in the face of the heaviest odds, who never turn their backs but march breast forward 'to do or die.'"[22]

The BSA's first publication salvo on the book front was *Every Boy's Library*. These books were reprints of classic literature for boys to "combat the menace of mediocrity and viciousness found in other cheap juveniles."[23] By November 1913 the BSA had published the first twenty-five titles of a series that would eventually grow to seventy-three books of "wholesome interest." Books by Robert Louis Stevenson, Jack London, James Fenimore Cooper, Beard, and Seton were included.

The second salvo was direct competition in Scout fiction. There were nine different series of Boy Scout adventures by 1914, but fanciful "Scout" stories about hot air balloons on the front in Germany and dog teams beyond the Arctic Circle were anathema to Mathiews and West. Mathiews hired Percy Keese Fitzhugh as the unofficial Scout fiction writer. His Tom Slade, Pee Wee Harris, Roy Blakeley, and the other Bridgeboro Scouts had wholesome adventures and utilized Scout skills in seventy-eight different books.[24] Paradoxically enough, the much maligned Scout fiction was able to buy advertising space in *Boys' Life* and Grosset and Dunlap, publisher of Every Boy's Library and the Fitzhugh series, noted on the dust jackets that "parents may select any of these Grosset and Dunlap books for their boys and girls and know that they are wholesome and clean in every way." "These books" included Tom Swift, the Hardy Boys, and the Rover Boys - series of which Mathiews did not approve.

To promote the right sort of recreational reading ("The Boy's Indoor Sport"), Mathiews introduced "Safety First Juvenile Book Week." This evolved into "Good Book Week" and finally "Children's Book Week" celebrated in early November at the beginning of the holiday book-buying season. Publishers supported the concept of buying more books but did nothing to screen the content.

Mathiews also presided over the first publication of a Boy Scout Bible, encouraged Scouts to spend Sundays after church reading, and lobbied for a merit badge in Bible Study. The Board turned down the latter suggestion. When the first Scout Song Book was published, Mathiews noted that the committee had gone over tens of thousands of songs to select those "that find the boy where he lives - without introducing the vulgar."[25] Of the resulting thirty songs, half had a Scouting sentiment and the rest were hymns.

Boys' Life was another front in the book war. The magazine published serials and stories "by writers who appreciate that the normal boy likes action."[26] A young man named Norman Rockwell was hired as an artist, and his first cover and two illustrations appeared in the September 1913 issue. West reported on "official news - what every Scout wants to know" - and profiled every recipient of medals for heroism and conservation. Dan Beard continued as Associate Editor for Handicraft. No one replaced Seton as Associate Editor for Nature but there were many nature articles by other men. A column of jokes, "Think and Grin," first appeared in June 1916. When Walter McGuire resigned as editor of *Boys' Life* to go to the *American Boy* in 1917, Mathiews replaced him as editor until West, himself, took over in 1923.

West clearly agreed with the Mathiews approach to reading. "Tell me what a boy reads and how he spends his leisure time and I can tell you what he will probably become. Boys who spend hours reading what is often called 'trash' - books that are carelessly written and inaccurate, books with characters that are not true to life - rarely develop into leaders. In later life they are incapable of forming clear, independent, judgments; they can be led about like sheep just as, when they were boys, the trash they read led them about like sheep."[27] It was recommended that every council in the country have a Reading Committee and develop an approved reading list. Some did. Furthermore, each and every troop was supposed to have a reading counselor. Most did not. The passion was primarily at the top. In fact, the whole book war was one-sided. The writers and publishers of other Scout fiction continued business as usual despite opposition from Mathiews and West.

A related skirmish in the war took place over the content of the newest entertainment medium - moving pictures. In 1915 the BSA endorsed and promoted a movie called variously *The Making of a Scout* or *The Adventures of a Boy Scout* in which a slum boy named Tom Slade was reformed by a scoutmaster and his troop and went on to do wonderful deeds. On the other hand, West succeeded in having an unnamed 1916 film recalled because "nothing in the film is accurately descriptive of the work of our Movement." The movie showed Scouts reviewed by officers carrying swords, sham battles, bayonet drills, and military maneuvers.[28] The search for the ideal motion picture would engage both Mathiews and West for the rest of their long careers.

Germany

After Congress declared war on Germany on April 5, 1917, Scouts adopted the slogan "Help Win the War!" Most of their service projects were noble and successful but some were not. A memo from the Office of Naval Intelligence indicated that, in addition to emergency coast watch, early in the war, Scouts were used to run down reports of unauthorized radio stations, gather information on enrolled men who had not reported for duty, and look into alleged cases of pro-German activity. In the Third Naval District in Brooklyn 125 cases were referred to the Scouts and the Scouts, initiated another 40 cases themselves. There was a similar report from the Fourth Naval District in Philadelphia. West approved.[29] These were not noble endeavors.

There was an appeal to patriotism as well as to Scout skills. For example:

> Here's another opportunity for boys to demonstrate their loyalty and their scouting ability. In accordance with an Executive Order issued by the President of the United States, it is illegal for any persons not authorized Government officials to operate a wireless plant or to have one in such condition as to be capable of operation. This applies to receiving as well as transmitting stations.

> Every Scout should dismantle his apparatus immediately.
> This means the taking down of the antenna wire, and
> the disconnecting and packing of the instruments.
>
> Scouts should not only dismantle their own apparatus,
> but report to the local police department any station
> aside from those they know to be Government stations
> which are in operation.[30]

An editorial entitled "If your Scoutmaster Leaves for Military Service" urged: "Our troop organization must be continued, said the Chief Scout Executive in a recent statement to all Scouts. Whenever our leaders enter active military service at the front, their places must be filled immediately from the ranks of the patriotic men who must stay at home because of those who are dependent upon them or because of physical disability. There will be no lack of leaders for the patriotic program of the Boy Scouts of America if the call for volunteers is issued in each locality as the needs develop."[31]

There were two exceptions to this patriotic call: Scout officials and German Scoutmasters. West asked for clarification of the Selective Draft requirement regarding exemptions for Scout officials. He learned that it was a Local Board decision. If he actively sought such exemptions, he did not publicize it. Germans were another matter. Scouting Magazine ordered:

> If there is a Hun in our ranks, give him the boot.
>
> Send his name and address to National Headquarters
> with evidence of his disloyalty [e.g. sluggish selling of
> Liberty Bonds and War Savings Stamps.]
>
> Our Constitution limits membership to American
> citizens and those who legally and otherwise have fully
> demonstrated their Americanism. We have no right to
> place American boys under other leadership.
>
> It is recognized that there are some exceptional cases
> where the motives are good, but in view of the present

> wartime conditions it is far better not to take chances.
> The safest course is not to permit German leadership
> in the work of the Boy Scouts of America.[32]

Scouts did perform remarkable service in selling United States Treasury Bonds. For the First Liberty Loan campaign, June 11 to 14, 1917, National Headquarters devised a campaign and a circular. Ten million circulars were printed, to that date the largest job ever handled by the Government Printing Office. The Scouts followed adult canvassers so they were called "gleaners after the reapers" in terms used in harvesting grain. The "gleaners" secured over $23 million in subscriptions. In the five Liberty Loans, the Scouts sold over $352 million worth of government bonds.[33]

The government also raised money through War Savings Stamps. Scouts dutifully went forth to sell stamps and were rewarded with over $101 million in sales.

Scouts worked with the Red Cross, local police, and other civic authorities. They served as government dispatch bearers and collected one hundred train carloads of peach pits. Actually, peach, apricot, prune, plum, olive, date, and cherry pits as well as the shells of Brazil, hickory, walnut, and butternuts were collected. This material was burned to form a high-grade charcoal used in gas masks. Seven pounds of pits or shells produced enough carbon for one mask. Scouts also undertook a national census of black walnut trees. Walnut was used for airplane propellers and gunstocks. In 1917 they distributed five thousand copies of President Wilson's Flag Day address. Mathiews urged the collection of books by "reputable authors" to be sent to soldiers.

One highly promoted campaign that was not particularly successful was the War Garden project. The rallying cry was, "Every Scout to feed a soldier." Scouts were encouraged to plant gardens for local consumption so that commercial production could be directed to the military. *Boys' Life* had several "how to do it" articles and the BSA sold rakes for 40 cents and hoes for 75 cents. (Express charges were extra.) One patriotic gardening slogan was "Woodchucks are pro-German." Shoot an enemy agent in your own backyard.

While thousands of boys could be mobilized for one-shot projects such as sales or surveys, months of planting, tending, and harvesting were apparently beyond the attention span of the average Scout. One hundred thousand circulars promoting Scout gardens were printed. Twelve thousand gardens were planted. Fewer than five hundred medals were awarded. The exact number was never published because it might have been perceived as a failed project. Most of these projects had a greater public relations potential than they did a practical use of Scout skills. Public relations that were good for Scouting were also good for James E. West.

According to educator James Russell;

> [Scouting] has marvelous potency for converting the restless, irresponsible, self-centered boy into the straightforward, dependable, helpful young citizen. To the boy who will give himself to it, there is plenty of work that looks like play, standards of excellence which he can appreciate, rules of conduct which he must obey, positions of responsibility which he may occupy as soon as he qualifies himself in a word, a program that appeals to a boy's instincts, and a method adapted to a boys nature.[34] . . . I venture to say that most scouts are in closer touch with their scoutmasters than they are with their school teachers, and know Mr. West better than they know their superintendent of schools or the state commissioner of education.[35]

West must have appreciated that.

President Woodrow Wilson issued a proclamation on May 1, 1919: "The Boy Scouts have not only demonstrated their worth to the Nation, but have also materially contributed to a deeper appreciation by the American people, of the higher conception of patriotism and good citizenship."[36] It was undoubtedly one of Scouting's finest hours. Wilson would go on to say, "It is fine to have the boys of the country organized for the purposes that the Boy Scouts represent, and whenever I see a group of them, I am proud of their manliness and feel cheered by the knowledge of what their organization represents."[37]

After the War

After the war, Scouts continued to provide community service, and West tried to keep the image of the well-uniformed, helpful Scout in the public eye. For example, Scouts provided first aid throughout the nation during the influenza epidemic, but that was quiet service.

On a grand scale, West was able to mobilize large numbers of Scouts for public occasions in New York City. There was a great rally in Central Park when Baden-Powell made his third visit to the United States in March 1919. In November of that year, West was able to mobilize 35,000 Scouts to wave flags for General Pershing. Scouts had an obligation to uphold standards, however. West editorialized:

> During the recent Red Cross parade, I with my family, had seats on the reviewing stand directly opposite the stand set aside for President Wilson. One scout who had been given the privilege of serving as usher in the stand caused me great mortification. He discarded his coat, his neckerchief, rolled up his shirt sleeves and allowed his trousers to hang down slovenly; he did not know enough to keep modestly out of the way, and, to make matters worse, he vigorously chewed gum. Of course, he was unconscious of the great harm he was doing to the Boy Scouts of America, but the harm was done just the same.[38]

Some steps were taken to refine the structure of Scout troops. Experience during the war had shown that when a Scoutmaster left, the troop frequently folded and it was further noted that not every Scoutmaster accepted "organizational goals" such as no military drill. "The Boy Scouts of America wisely took steps to place upon the institutions the responsibility, as a necessary step incident to the organization of a Troop, of the selection of a committee of members of the institution . . . [to] certify and stand in for the Scoutmaster and insure harmony with the aims and purposes of the institution."[39] The Troop Committee helped the Scoutmaster who still received the charter. The National Council also decided to limit the size of a troop to four patrols of eight boys, believing that that was as many as one Scoutmaster could handle. The idea of an Assistant Scoutmaster came later and the practice of giving the charter to the institution and not the Scoutmaster was not formalized until 1935.

One problem that had been obvious since Scouting began was that boys didn't stay in the program very long. Using the slogan "Once a Scout, Always a Scout," West introduced a number of retention schemes. An "Associate Scout" could attend as few as one meeting a year. A "Veteran Scout" with five years tenure could register without cost. "Pioneer Scouts" could enroll without belonging to a Troop. None of these schemes was particularly successful.

James E. West had once been the only professional Scout Executive. As more First Class Councils hired executives, West perceived the need for training and supervision, not only in New York City, but in field offices throughout the country as well. By 1916 it was clear that this new profession of Scouting needed standards and organization so West convened the first Conference of Scout Executives at National Headquarters on May 17th. Thirty-nine Scout officials attended. The next day the group had lunch at the Atlantic Yacht Club on Long Island. "In the afternoon, the visitors were entertained at the home of Scout Executive James E. West, where an informal program of scout games was followed. Tea was served by Mrs. West, assisted by the wives of the National Headquarters staff."[40] A second conference was held in 1918, but the major work of professional development would not take place until the next decade.

The Boy Scouts of America actually had a small financial surplus at the end of 1918. The Executive Board was happy enough with West's performance that they increased his salary from $6,000 to $7,500 per year.[41] Financially, the "Period of Individual Solicitation" had given way to the "Period of Large Scale Mass Campaigns."[42] Large scale solicitations by mail and telegram were moderately successful but extremely time-consuming. The organization would have to find a better way to finance the program. At the end of the decade (December 31, 1919), membership (Scouts and Scouters) stood at 462,781. 9.4 % of American boys twelve to nineteen were enrolled.

Teddy Roosevelt

Teddy Roosevelt died on January 6, 1919. As far as West was concerned, the Chief Scout Citizen was more useful dead than alive. His credentials were impeccable. In addition to being Chief Scout Citizen, Roosevelt had been Honorary Vice-President of the Boy Scouts of America, Scout Commissioner for Nassau County, and a Committee Member of Troop 39 at Christ Church in Oyster Bay, New York. He admired Scouting and said wonderful things about it, but he was militaristic and nationalistic and would rather go hunting than attend a meeting. He was usually too busy to write the articles, make the speeches, or endorse the projects that West wanted him to do. It was far simpler, then, for West to use an old picture of Roosevelt and quote him when an endorsement of Scouting was needed. West could use that part of a speech that he liked: "The Boy Scout Movement is distinctly as asset to our country for the development of efficiency, virility, and good citizenship" and ignore the rest: "It is essential that its leaders be men of strong, wholesome character, of unmistakable devotion to our country, its customs, and ideals, as well as in soul and by law citizens thereof, whose whole-hearted loyalty is given to this nation and to this nation alone," if it sounded too nativistic.[43]

In October 1919 Dan Beard led about 250 Scouts on a memorial pilgrimage to Roosevelt's grave. This pilgrimage became an annual event on the Saturday nearest Roosevelt's birthday of October 27, and it would soon draw thousands of Scouts from the Northeast. Acorns from nearby oaks and nuts from a black walnut near the grave were distributed so that Scouts could plant "Roosevelt trees" throughout the country. West wrote, "I will go further and suggest that every Boy Scout and indeed every American boy who aspires to be a manly man, arrange individually to plant a memorial Roosevelt tree."[44]

West promoted such historic pilgrimages not only to the grave of Roosevelt in Oyster Bay, but also to those of Washington at Mount Vernon, and Lincoln in Springfield, Illinois as well as to those of less well-known Presidents such as Millard Fillmore in Buffalo, New York and Franklin Pierce in Concord, New Hampshire. He wanted to honor all the presidents, but he also wanted the Scouts to be seen honoring all the presidents.

Family

For the West family, the decade had been one of growth and tragedy. After a serious bout with pneumonia, young Jimmie West died of a seizure disorder on November 14, 1916, while Marion West was pregnant with their fourth child. West's response to the death of his eldest son and namesake has not been recorded. Arthur had been born in 1912, Marion in 1914, Helen in 1916, and Bob in 1917. The family had also moved from Forest Hills to the Sea Gate area of Brooklyn where West was an active member of the Playground Committee. Unfortunately, there are no family records of the early years, and Helen was to young to remember them.

Notes

1 Beard Library of Congress (LOC) 129 6/12/16

2 Beard LOC 129 12/05/16

3 Beard LOC 129 1/20/17

4 Beard LOC 129 1/15/17

5 Beard LOC 130 4/17/18

6 Beard LOC 130 9/13/18

7 Beard LOC 130 2/19/19

8 West in Proceedings of 2nd National Training Conference (NTC) 1922 page 354

9 West page 355

10 Ibid

11 *Wo-He-Lo: The Camp Fire History.* Campfire, Inc. 1980

12 Gulick Archives, Springfield College

13 From *Today's Magazine* 6/15/12 in Gulick Archives

14 West page 354

15 West page 356

16 Beard LOC 130

17 Proceedings of 2nd NTC, 1922 page 180

18 Fourth Annual Report of the BSA page 63

19 *The Outlook* 11/18/14 page 652

20 Sixth Annual Report of the BSA page 61

21 Fourth Annual Report of the BSA page 61

22 Ibid page 64

23 Ibid page 62

24 See Dizer, J. *Tom Swift, The Bobbsey Twins, and Other Heroes of American Juvenile Literature.* Lewiston, NY: Edward Mellon Press, 1997

25 *Scout Executive* 10/20 page 33

26 *Boys' Life* 7/12 page 16

27 *Boys' Life* 11/33 page 20

28 *Scouting* 7/15/16 page 3

29 Beard LOC 129 9/06/17 memo

30 *Boys' Life* 6/17 page 43

31 Ibid page 42

32 *Scouting* 8/15/17 page 8

33 See Murray,Wm. *The History of the Boy Scouts of America.* New York: BSA, 1937 page 106 ff

34 Russell, James E. "Scouting education" in *Educational Review* 6/17 page 7

35 Ibid page 11

36 Murray, page 132

37 *Boys' Life* 5/17 page 21

38 *Boys' Life* 7/18 page 30

[39] Scouting 3/29 page 82
[40] Scouting 6/11/16 page 5
[41] Beard LOC 130 minutes
[42] See Murray
[43] "Statement by Colonel Roosevelt" originally quoted in Scouting 8/15/17 page 8
[44] Boys' Life 3/39 page 28

Chapter 5

The Twenties

Interchangeable Executives

If the teens were the decade in which the BSA defined itself, then the twenties were the decade when it became standardized. By 1920 most of the original boys' workers who founded the movement and served on its first Executive Board had been replaced by businessmen who were content to let the experts manage the details. In 1919 Charles Jackson of Boston had suggested that a famous man such as Theodore Roosevelt be paid to serve as an active President of the Board. To this West responded, "Can there be more than one head in any organization?"[1]

His vision of the Executive Board was most clearly articulated by West in a later address to Scout Executives with regard to their own local boards: "The function of the Volunteer is not to dominate over the Executive, for he, the Executive, is essential. There must be a head who is responsible. The Volunteer is not administrative. That must be done by the head. The Executive must be held responsible to the Board for the operations of the work of the Movement . . . [but] we must not in our success lose sight of the fact that we always have been, and increasingly, we are always going to be dependent upon the place that the man of affairs, the man of active business and educational connections has with the Boy Scout Movement."[2]

While the progressive vision focused on solving the moral problems of capitalism, progressive leaders such as West brought the capitalists on board to support his social agenda. These men were familiar with the role of a Board of Directors and a movement that embraced the Protestant work ethic and middle class values could only have appealed to them. The corporate class needed the middle class as consumers in order to make the corporate economy work. They liked West's pro-business thinking and professionalism. "Professionalism" itself, is a middle class value.[3]

The Executive Board acknowledged that West was in charge. When Milton McRae, an original member of the Board, introduced West as "the greatest boy worker in the United States" at an address in San Diego, California on January 31, 1920, he noted that "the Chief Scout Executive really directs the Movement; we counsel with him, we advise him, but he is the factor - he is the pivot on which all the machinery turns. And he is giving his life to it. When I tell you that he spoke seven times yesterday at seven different meetings you can imagine the work he has been doing."[4]

At the end of 1919, there were 7850 troops with 185,000 boys in organized councils and an additional 175,000 boys in 8326 troops, primarily in rural areas, who reported directly to the National Council. This was quite a burden on the national office. "These troops are not only dependent upon the national office for the purchase of their badges, literature, and other supplies, but present all sorts of problems which require patient and careful handling, and necessitate a great volume of correspondence."[5]

West rose to the administrative challenge. He established perfor-mance incentives in the form of higher wages, and, with training for the clerical, recording, and stenographic forces, West could proudly report ".00076 percent of errors in a total of 3,683,726 transactions" in 1919.[6]

Efficiency was important. Suggestions for local council offices ap-plied to the national office as well. Standardized equipment and orderly desks and files were important. "Tidy desks vouch much for the efficiency of the ones using them."[7] This even included recommendations for what was to be kept in each desk drawer. There was a table of organization for the office staff and a schedule for each person. Results could not be measured without records. Records could not be kept without forms. Forms had to be specific, and 48 different ones were suggested.[8] Every employee was requested to read the Constitution and By-laws of the Boy Scouts of America twice a year.

Despite this increased efficiency, it soon became obvious to the

Executive Board that the number of units reporting directly to the national office in New York City had to be reduced. They started with the troops in New York itself and determined to establish separate councils in each of the five boroughs in the city. Some borough councils had been organized as early as 1910, but the National Council dissolved them in 1918 in a disagreement over funding issues.[9] In 1921 West led a delegation to the office of a young lawyer named Franklin D. Roosevelt and persuaded him to chair a Greater New York Foundation which would oversee all the borough councils. Roosevelt agreed only "if there was no work attached."[10] He may have been one of the first people to be told that Scouting "takes only one hour a week," because he accepted the job.

Throughout the rest of the country, the concept of an "area" rather than a "city" council evolved as the local councils took over the responsibility of service to the individual units. Each council would provide camping opportunities, review boards called "Courts of Honor" to establish common standards of achievement, leadership training, and a local community identity.[11] They would also be able to sell badges and literature. While some volunteer Commissioners in second class councils performed exceedingly well, it was clear that if trained professionals were in charge of each council, then a standardized program could be delivered.

As early as 1914 the national office had employed Field Secretaries to aid in the organization of local councils. By 1918 there were eight of them, but the entire country was not yet organized. The man who did that was Dr. George J. Fisher.

Fisher started boys' work as physical director of the Cincinnati YMCA. "He was among the first physical directors to recognize the advantage of a medical education as a means of rightly guiding the well, rather than as a means of ministering to men after the neglect of health has brought them to beds of sickness."[12] After he received his MD from the University of Cincinnati in 1898, Fisher followed Luther Gulick as Director of Physical Training for the International Committee of the YMCA. During World War I, he served as director of recreation and athletics for the YMCA National War Work Council where he was credited with originating the game of volleyball. Volleyball remained his passion as he edited the Official Volleyball Guide for twenty-one years and organized the United States Volleyball Association.[13] Fisher had been a Scouting volunteer since 1910 when he chaired the Committee on Badges, Awards, and Scout Requirements. He wrote the chapter on "Health and Endurance" for the 1911 Handbook. In 1919 West actively recruited Fisher for a new job: Deputy Chief Scout Executive and Director of the Field Department. West wrote, "I am full of joy in anticipation of what it will mean to the Boy Scouts of America to have benefit of Dr. Fisher's services."[14] Harold Pote, later the Director of Personnel, described it as an ideal pairing. Fisher was a diplomat, a negotiator, and a compromiser who often had to smooth the feathers that West had ruffled with his gruff, goal-oriented manner. Fisher was at ease with people, confident in himself, and one of the few people who could convince West that there were alternative ways to accomplish some things.[15]

In 1920 the Five-Year Field Program began. The grand plan was to organize the entire country (the "field") into local councils, perhaps as many as 1343. Large areas could logically be divided into as many as 3573 districts serving different trade centers within each council. Regional offices would serve the councils. Twelve regions, "following somewhat the geographical lines of the Federal Reserve Bank System area"[16] were established. The regions have never been independent and function as administrative divisions or branches of the national office. The Regional Executive and Regional Committees were charged with extending the Council Plan throughout the region and promoting the "Quota Plan" of local council contributions to the national budget. Each council was to pay one dollar per 1000 enrolled Scouts plus a seventy-five dollar charter fee. If a council met its quota, the National Council would not try to raise money in competition with the local council within its service area. For 1921 of 290 first class councils, 198 accepted and paid their quota, thirty negotiated partial payment, sixty-one deferred payment, and one refused. This quota fee from the councils, along with individual registration fees (raised from twenty-five cents to fifty cents in 1921), royalties, sales income, and contributions established financial stability for the BSA. The most important of the contributions was a $500,000 special fund of which $100,000 came from Executive Board member Mortimer Schiff of Kuehn and Loeb.

In 1922 Schiff offered to pay the annual $6,000 salary of one Field

Executive in each region if the region would match it. All regions did and the process of extension and organization was accelerated. At the end of the five years, the process was nearly complete. By the end of the decade there were over 630 local councils, only one of which (Panama Canal Zone) was still headed by a volunteer.

With the rapidly growing number of paid field executives, it was soon obvious that standardized training of these men would be necessary. The first of what were to become Biennial Conferences of Scout Executives was held at Bear Mountain, New York in 1920. Two hundred field executives attended. The proceedings were published in a new magazine, *The Scout Executive*, of which Fisher was editor. Another result of the meeting was the first manual for executives, *Community Boy Leadership*, which was published in 1921.

An organization that suggested how to arrange desk drawers would not shy away from defining "the culture of the Scout Executive." Qualifications for a Scouting professional included character, executive ability, personality, technical ability, education, business ability, and social vision.[17] The Scout Executive should read a daily newspaper, a weekly news digest, book reviews, and at least one book a month, including great literature such as the Harvard Classics. He should do in-depth reading or take courses in a related topic such as psychology or business, and he should attend conferences and summer schools.[18]

There is no identified author of *Community Boy Leadership*, but several points near and dear to West were made in this manual:

> Scouting is a profession for the Scout Executive, because of the vital social quality of the work of serving the community, through the art of character building, companionship, and leadership of its boyhood.[19]
>
> * * *
>
> No man merits consideration who does not have a positive religious tone and recognizedly [sic] high moral quality on which the other needed qualities of leadership are to be builded. [sic] Only he can hope to train a child in the way to go who goes that way himself. The moral quality of the profession is therefore basic and imperative.[20]

* * *

The Scout Executive is primarily a <u>man's man</u>, whose work it is to mobilize men and forces in the community to serve and train boyhood.[21] [The Scoutmaster would provide boys with] character building companionship.[22]

* * *

As a commissioned officer of the Boy Scouts of America he shall serve as the representative of the National Council in the responsibility of maintaining standards[23] [Therefore,] he has no right to tangentially diverge as long as he bears the Scout label.[24]

* * *

[Like his staff, he should have] definite annual or monthly objectives [and] analyze out how he spends his business time, recreation time, study or growth time, etc., so as to know the facts and be able to correct poor balance or actual wastage of time.[25]

The executive manual said nothing about traditional Scout skills or Scoutcraft. With the emphasis on business practice, reading, high moral standards, and efficiency, the Chief Scout Executive was creating a profession in his own image. They were leaders of men, not outdoorsmen.

West went so far as to caution Scout Executives against being Scoutmasters:

> Surely he must not have personal relations to individual boys by which he gives to them a special service or special privileges. There is a practice, among some executives, fortunately true of very few, but nevertheless true of those few, who take individual boys on trips, often away overnight, sometimes occupying the same room in a hotel. This an executive, no matter how well meaning he may be, should not do. It lays him open to criticism. It is not a proper relation. It is too personal, too intimate, too discriminating. It is not wise. We cannot be too emphatic on this point.[26]

Reading assignments and attendance at national conferences became part of the organizational requirements. Dr. Elbert K. Fretwell, Dean of the Teachers' College at Columbia University, was instrumental in organizing the second Executive Conference in 1922. The proceedings, including the presentations and, especially, the "Problem Hours" with West's verbatim responses to questions from the floor provide valuable insight into how the organization developed. Each session would "afford opportunity to discuss any policy or step in the routine procedure of the Boy Scouts of America, in order that there may be a full and frank consideration of the subject on its merits, with a view to recommending modification if analysis and discussion show it to be advisable."[27]

This 1922 Conference was held at Blue Ridge, North Carolina and 293 of 418 field executives attended. The conference was highlighted by the presentation of a gold Eagle badge to Dan Beard. In making the presentation, West said, "All of us here, by sharing an equal part, have provided this solid gold Eagle Scout badge, the only one that has ever been made, and the only one bestowed, to be presented on this occasion in recognition of our high regard for him and of his services to the boyhood of the world."[28] The presentation did not prevent Beard from complaining further about West.

There were 499 Scout executives at the 1924 Conference in Estes Park, Colorado, 708 at the 1926 session in Hot Springs, Arkansas, and 799 in Ithaca, New York in 1928. In November 1925 forty-three men attended the first thirty-day training school for new field executives at the Bear Mountain Inn. Several schools were held each year after that and, after 1927, all newly hired executives had to attend.

As Chief Scout Executive, West traveled to executive conferences and many other events. In early 1923 he made a typical 12,000 mile trip where he spoke at five regional meetings, stopped in twenty-two cities and addressed 10,000 men and 30,000 boys. In San Francisco a Scout band met him at the station, and a parade headed by Eagle Scouts and with prominent city and Scout officials acting as escorts led him to a rally where he spoke to 5,000 Scouts. In Utah he addressed the state legislature, and in Idaho he met the governor.[29] Some years he traveled as many as 40,000 miles. He spoke to service clubs, Scout groups and high school assemblies, attended Scout rallies, Scout circuses, and Scout camps, and presented Eagle badges and awards for heroism.

At one rally, Raymond O. Hanson noted:

> A tremendous ovation greeted Mr. West as he stepped
> forward to make his address. In the more than
> fifteen years that I have known the Big Chief, I have
> seen and heard many tributes paid to him and his
> accomplishments, but never have I witnessed a more
> touching and striking tribute to any man than that
> which came spontaneously from the crowd at the close
> of Mr. West's address. After relating the struggles of his
> boyhood, the later experiences of his young manhood,
> and how these elements in the foundation of his life
> had enabled him to give of his best to the leadership
> of the boyhood of America, there was a new light of
> understanding and of courage in the sea of upturned
> faces, and throughout the auditorium scouts rose to
> their feet as one boy in a mighty cheer for the man who
> embodied in his own life an experience, the highest
> ideals and purposes of our Movement.[30]

Consolidation of Power

By 1923 *Boys' Life* was in trouble. Circulation was far below
membership and the magazine was losing money. The Business Director thought that the BSA should sell it. West refused. He had to have
regular communication with Scouts to deliver his program of character
development and citizenship training. He persuaded the Laura Spellman Rockefeller Foundation to lend the magazine $100,000 with a line
of credit for an additional $100,000. Frank Presbrey, Chairman of the
Editorial Board, essentially agreed to take a personal mortgage so that
the BSA would be free of any financial obligation, but the Foundation
would be reimbursed if the magazine could not repay the loan. West
took over as Editor. In his first edition, West wrote an open letter to
Presbrey: "It is with a very deep sense of my responsibility, and a keen
appreciation of the great things that are ahead for *Boys' Life*, that I have
agreed to accept the Editorship of the magazine, which begins its big
new policy of improvement and expansion with the October number.
I am proud to give my best to this wonderful work."[31] The changes

appeared to be minimal, as Dan Beard added a new column where he answered questions from Scouts and West wrote more editorials. Nevertheless, the changes were successful as the magazine borrowed a total of $151,000 and made enough profit to repay it.[32]

Not everyone recognized the growing consolidation of power in West's office as a good thing, however. As early as 1914 Arthur Carey protested that the organization was "too highly centralized; thereby making administration very expensive and inconvenient and depriving individual localities of the sense of self-governing communities" and that the subsequent expense required fund-raising with "recourse to commercial methods not in accordance with the spirit of chivalry as conveyed in the Scout Law."[33] That same year, the Bureau of Municipal Research issued a report on the BSA. In part, the report noted that "the internal organization of the national headquarters is that of a well-planned administrative unit. The scout executive in charge has given careful consideration to the many problems of office management. The procedure of each department as been definitized along simple but effective lines, and the work of the several units has been properly correlated. Rules and regulations have been promulgated covering every important detail of clerical and office routine. As a result, a high degree of institutional and individual efficiency has been secured." The report actually equated this with the organizational efficiency and impersonality of Sears and Roebuck.[34]

Standardized training produced a standardized product. Scout executives had more loyalty to the national office than to their own local area. Most of the men were now college graduates and solidly middle-class. With more frequent transfer and promotion, they were also interchangeable. As Mcleod noted, "The BSA's administrative system built in conservatism, for men who had to enforce standard requirements, wanted them kept simple and stable."[35]

One real innovation in the midst of organizational bureaucracy was the formation of the Scout Executives Alliance in 1920. Participant contributions provided one of the first death benefit plans in the United States. It was even tapped on occasion, especially during the Depression, to help employees who had not contributed to the plan.[36] There was also discussion of starting a retirement plan, but the major hurdle was funding for executives employed before the start of the plan. It would be another decade before that problem was solved.

The British were critical of the American system and its professional service. Baden-Powell thought that Scouting should be managed by volunteers. In fact, two-thirds of his commissioners were retired military men on pensions and/or minor aristocrats and B-P never appeared to appreciate that Scouting might be different in other countries from what it was in Britain. According to Pote, Baden-Powell often referred disparagingly to West's "big office" and its emphasis on "typewriters and figures."[37] Surprisingly, Baden-Powell had written West in 1916 that "[your] success has been due to the skill with which your Council and your workers have adapted the idea to American conditions and have made the best possible development of it."[38] It is not clear when he changed his mind.

When Baden-Powell's Deputy, Captain Francis Gidney, visited the United States in 1923-1924, he thought that the paid executives were doing a good job given the "work culture" of the country:

> On coming to this country, first of all I must confess a certain surprise that it should be necessary to have so many whole-time workers, and one rather wondered at the wisdom of such action when comparing your method with ours in England. However, after my experience here, I can see that comparisons are odious, as the conditions are so vastly different. We in England are fortunate in having a large number of high-grade men who have made their mark in their various professions and are anxious to take up leadership in the Scout Movement is a voluntary way. It is a national characteristic of the average Englishman to look forward to the time when he can retire on a moderately comfortable income. This he usually does at about 45 to 50 years of age, and when he has retired, seeks for some worthwhile occupation to keep him busy and interested, as he is naturally still a man full of life. The natural tendency, on the other hand, for the average American citizen is, that the more successful he becomes in business, the more does he become tied up with activities and responsibilities of every sort and description. I think I am right in saying that he nearly always 'dies in harness.'

In the case of this country, therefore, where voluntary leadership is not available in the same measure, the only alternative to do the thing well, is to have whole-time men who make Scouting a life work. I must say that, considering the rapid growth of the Movement in this country, it is extraordinary what a high standard of character exists among the executives.[39]

Gidney also suggested that the BSA needed a national training center and programs for both younger and older boys as well.

In early 1926, Baden-Powell came to the United States for the fourth time. He visited Washington, D.C., Louisville, Kentucky, Kansas City, Chicago, Detroit, and New York City. The Chief Scout Executive accompanied him. On May 15, 1926 West wrote to then-Executive Board President Walter Head[40] about Baden-Powell:

He has been most generous and kind to me personally, but it does disappoint me considerably that in the entire time we were together, notwithstanding the many opportunities he had, he has yet to make one single reference to his appreciation of the part I have had and now have in the Boy Scout Movement here in America; in fact his attitude has been that of regarding us here as the other executives with whom he comes in contact as so many 'hired men,' but very fortunately, and I am so proud of this, I have been able to accept all of this situation without any rancor or pique, and it has not in the least interfered with my trying to figuratively 'turn the other cheek' and keep on smiling and going forward.

Tomorrow I celebrate my fiftieth birthday, and notwithstanding all I shall try to do if the usual happens, it will mean a time of looking backward and looking forward, in meditation, some 'blue moments,' but out of it all will come a consciousness of the great opportunity I have to serve, and I hope a determination to more effectively serve.[41]

The Twenties

This appears to be the essence of West - a social reformer eager to right the wrongs he had seen in his youth and a powerful intellectual with a nagging insecurity that he tried to overcome with bureaucratic efficiency and an autocratic attitude. Despite this, he truly seemed to believe that he was working for the boy. As he had written to Beard on May 7, 1921: "I have a great deal to learn yet. I want to invest all the strength and power I have along lines and in such a way as will be most helpful for making real red-blooded American men out of boys; men who appreciate the great out-of-doors, know how to take care of themselves and whose character has been so definitely developed as to give them a rudder and conscience which will carry them through any storm."[42] West constantly pointed to the Scout statue on his desk and said that all the decisions that he made were determined by considering "first, last, and all the time the boy." "Always, before making important decisions that will affect the lives of boys in Scouting, or those not directly influenced by the Movement, my eyes are drawn irresistibly for guidance and inspiration to the McKenzie statuette of the Boy Scout on my desk, because that heroic little bronze figure symbolizes to me the boyhood, not only in America but throughout the world, to whom, both by design and desire, I have dedicated the utmost of my ability."[43] West also had a statuette in the main stairwell at home so that he had to pass it at least twice a day.[44] He had multiple opportunities to consult his muse.

Livingstone commended West in 1923: "I have never yet met a man whose manliness, whose loyalty to ideals, and whose faithfulness to friends, whether they be in trouble or not, is exceeded by what I have so long known and recognized to be your fundamental characteristics . . . Men in Scouting may come and go, but no man in Scouting will ever leave upon the pages of its history a more enviable record than that of your good self. Everything else you sacrificed to the interest of the Movement and that for which it stands the boyhood of America."[45]

Despite his golden Eagle award, Beard continued to snipe at West and his authority. In a June 4, 1925 letter he drafted for incoming Board President James J. Storrow, he wrote:

> In the first place, the Chief Scout Executive is appointed
> by the Board, or is supposed to be each year, and unless

he is he legally holds no office. He is not a member of
the Board, and has no right to vote nor speak without
permission. He was not 'brought down to act as
Chief Scout Executive,' he was not 'dragged into the
Movement,' he came eagerly to accept the position as
Secretary to the Board. I was there at the time. I was there
before it happened. The title 'Chief Scout Executive' had
not yet been invented, he worked it in gradually until
now he writes his own press releases, prints his own
pictures, sends them out to the papers announcing
himself as 'head of the Boy Scouts of America.' He has
literally taken possession of the Organization, of which
he is only an employee. He tells the different members of
the Executive Board what they must do, and the funny
part of it is many of them do it. He is not the type of
man that is popular among men or boys. For the Lord
sake, when you get into office get a tight grip of the reins,
use a curbed bit and let all our employees know that
you are the President of the Boy Scouts of America, the
Executive officer of the governing board which decides
all questions of policy and of finances, and is not to
be influenced by the politics of a paid force, which by
the way, is a magnificent lot of men whom I admire as
employees not as governors.

There is no trouble with the Boy Scouts, they are alright.
The Organization is splendid, but the egotism and
patent medicine advertisement of the personality of
the Executive is out of place, does nothing to promote
Scouting itself, and is offensive to thousands of good
men whom we need. Nevertheless, he is a good lobbyist,
a good organizer, and a useful man if someone will keep
him in his place.[46]

West had to be aware of Beard's comments, but, to his credit, he
never showed disrespect for the old man nor chastised him publicly.
West had previously written to Beard, "My task is most difficult under the most favorable conditions, and if by chance I do act in a way that
gives basis for a suspicion that I might wish to dominate, can't you

accept my assurances that such is not my intention? It is my intention, however, to discharge my responsibility and give leadership wherever I think it may be helpful, but I will never be guilty of participating, or approve of anybody else participating in any method that does not frankly and squarely develop differences of opinion so that the issues may be settled by those who have the authority and responsibility for settling them."[47] Beard characteristically wrote "BUNK" in the margins of such letters.

Beard's complaints about West's management style apparently concerned enough other Executive Board members that they commissioned the Mark Jones Report to look at the entire administrative structure of the BSA. The Rockefeller Foundation supported this three-year study (1926-1928). Unfortunately, no actual copies of this report appear to have survived. West was initially supportive and met with Jones on a weekly basis to try to influence him; however, Jones was still critical of the organization. He praised the Boy Scouts of America for its work with boys but criticized the national office for being too rigid and uncompromising and West for doing too much. "The manner in which he [the Chief Scout Executive] works causes him to do so with a degree of centralization that is much greater than we have found to be the case in any other comparable organization of which we have knowledge... It is evident to us from our study of National Headquarters that the overconcentration of work at the Chief Scout Executive's desk is a basic problem of Scouting."[48] (Twenty-four department heads reported directly to West.) Jones recommended that the National Executive Board be expanded and meet five times per year and that a smaller Executive Committee meet monthly. He suggested a ten million dollar extension campaign as well as programs for older and younger boys.[49]

West responded to the report by chairing the Committee on Implementation and, three years later, he appointed a Cabinet consisting of himself, his Deputy, and the Directors of the Divisions of Program, Personnel, Operations, and Business. On the surface, it appeared that West had responded to Jones' major criticism and decentralized the organization. Major field organization was now complete and the twelve regional directors reported to the Division of Operations, and Fisher now devoted all his energy within the national office. Instead of twenty-four reports, West now dealt with only five; however, he still approved every decision and remained firmly in control.

West at Home

If the Jones Report is difficult to find, then information about the "Home Fund" is nearly impossible to locate. Early in the decade, West reminded the Board that when he moved up from Washington, he was promised a home appropriate to his status as Chief Executive. Discussions about a home were apparently carried on in those parts of the meeting where "Other matters will be brought to the attention of the Board informally." The Board resolved to raise $50,000, but collected only $26,600. West had to take a $30,000 mortgage to cover the purchase and renovations. Schiff gave $5,000 toward the project in 1924. Although sometimes critical of West, Schiff needed his support to become Board President whenever Livingstone stepped down.

Around 1922 West, his wife Marion, and the children Arthur, Marion, Helen, and Bob had moved from Sea Gate to Pelham. In August 1926 West announced that they had moved into a large home at 1224 North Avenue (later renumbered as 1338) in New Rochelle, New York. They were welcomed by the local Siwanoy Council, which presented West with a council pin and a flag and gave Mrs. West an azalea bush. West told the readers of *Boys' Life*, "It was an official welcome to the city of New Rochelle, to our new home, which is a story in itself and which I hope to tell you someday."[50] He never did explain the financing. The Wests then employed a black couple, "my man" Richard as driver and handyman, and Annabell as cook and maid. Annabell wore a uniform.

Given his own medical history, West was aware of then current theories of the role of fresh air and fresh vegetables in the prevention of tuberculosis. He applied them to his children. They slept out on a sleeping porch during the summer and fall, and a gardener was employed. The children joked about "fifty cent lima beans" because of his salary. Bob raised chickens. His father bought the feed and also paid Bob for the eggs. Mrs. West made currant jelly and baked Parker House rolls. To Helen, it felt like a warm family home.

Without a real childhood of his own, it must have been very difficult for West to be a parent. He was distant and rarely smiled. "The orphanage downgraded him and took all the joy out of his life." There was discipline. Dinner was served promptly at six and was always in abundance. Everyone was required to report "what have you done for God and family today" before grace. "Dad put up a chart and we had to grade ourselves on things like making the beds, emptying the baskets, and deportment." Punishment was administered in the second floor bathroom. West would spank the children lightly for misbehavior or wash their mouths out with soap for swearing. "We knew what we had done wrong."[51]

On Sundays the family attended services and Sunday School at the North Avenue Presbyterian Church. Afterward, West would take the family for a ride in the Packard. Helen describes this as "quite an experience," as West would yell at anyone who littered. After the drive, they would call Wilson's Drug to send over ice cream.

The girls walked to grade school and high school while the boys prepped at Phillips Andover and Phillips Exeter. Helen always wrote her father's occupation as "Chief Scout Executive of the Boy Scouts of America" "because it was important to acknowledge that."[52]

West "poured himself wholly into what he was doing." After dinner he went to his home office to smoke a cigar and deal with the full briefcase that he had brought home. He did not spontaneously reach out to his children but would put an arm around Helen if she climbed into his lap. He was proud of his family and their achievements. He took them to meetings and conferences, (Helen collected pennies at the door of the 1920 Executive Conference until her father made her stop) and a family photo was always on his Christmas card. The family always had a dog.

Arthur West became a Scout in 1925. He attended Dan Beard's summer camp in Pennsylvania in the summer of 1926 and earned his Second Class badge there. West proudly wrote Beard in follow-up. "Arthur is working on Archery and Bugling. We found it necessary to ask him to do his bugling practice on the third floor."[53] Arthur became a Patrol Leader in December. "He is enjoying his Scout experience very much, but I am afraid his Scoutmaster is not placing very much emphasis upon the Scout oath and law, the Daily Good Turn, and the ideals of service."[54] Arthur returned to Beard's camp in 1927 (at one-third off). Because of illness, he had to attend summer school in 1928 so that his sister would not catch up with him. West was clearly proud of his son. The only photograph in the 1927 pamphlet, "The Father and Son Idea in Scouting" is captioned "The Chief Scout Executive with his Scout pal and oldest son." Bobby also joined Troop 10 in New Rochelle in 1930, the year that Arthur was "Mayor" of the city on Anniversary Day, the day during Scout Week when Scouts took over the municipal offices. Both boys would go on to earn the Eagle rank. Neither Marion nor Helen ever expressed any interest in joining the Girl Scouts or Camp Fire Girls. All the children seemed to sense what was expected of them.

West wore an orthopedic shoe and brace but never spoke about his health or physical pain. His daughter referred to her mother as a "silent partner," "regal," and "with an inner light" never the "lady of the manor." She was conciliatory in public and never argued with her husband in front of the children, but they were known to exchange heated words after the children had gone to bed for the night. Publicly, Mrs. West was very supportive and seemed to play the same role of "smoothing ruffled feathers" in the community that Fisher played in the office.

Mother's family played an important role in the lives of the West children. Her brother, "Uncle Charlie," and his wife, Tanya, were frequent visitors. Tanya and her mother were Russian aristocrats who had escaped to Paris prior to the Revolution. She met Colonel Speaks in Paris during World War I and came to the United States with him. Her mother was a grandmother figure to the children and they called her "Nana." She played with them and told them stories of Imperial Russia.

The Chief relaxed by going to the club. In 1925 he joined the Wyckagill Country Club and in 1930 upgraded to the Westchester Country Club. He also belonged to the University Club in Washington and the Union League Club in New York City. The children, and later the grandchildren, swam at the Westchester Club but West neither golfed nor swam. Always supportive in public, Mrs. West did not swim because her husband did not. West was a country club officer at a time when the Club apparently admitted neither blacks nor Jews. As he advised local councils, he too accepted local customs.

Competition may have been a motivating factor for West. His brother-in-law Charles Speaks was President of Fisk Tire and set an example of conspicuous consumption as did his wife Tanya. Arthur's father-in-law was a construction magnate in upstate New York and owned several miles of Lake George waterfront. Both set high standards for spending, and West tried to live the same life-style.

West was driven to the station each morning where the New York Central allegedly waited until he was aboard. He did not waste time on the train. "I do make it my business to read two newspapers [each day]. I commute back and forth to New York and can get, enroute to my office and enroute home, an opportunity to get two extreme points of view editorially, and I like the editorials. I haven't very much sympathy with the policy of one of the papers, the ideals for which the paper stands, but reading its editorials does give me an experience in thinking, and I recommend it."[55] West took a cab from Grand Central to and from the office, and one observer was amazed at how easily he did it. "He would walk out, raise his cane in the air, and a cab would be there."[56] On one occasion, he phoned Mayor LaGuardia's office to stop noisy construction in front of his building.[57] That enhanced his reputation as a man who could get things done.

The World

After 1920, Baden-Powell focused on the international expansion of Scouting. The first World Jamboree was held in London that year. The United States sent a large contingent but Beard had not been invited to be a formal representative because West was afraid that he would say something derogatory about "foreigners." Beard went anyway and managed to hold his tongue. At the Jamboree Baden-Powell presented the Honorary Silver Wolf, the highest award in British Scouting, to West and Livingstone. Notice of this never appeared in BSA publications. Perhaps West did not want to call attention to himself in this way, or perhaps he was afraid that Beard would call him "Unamerican." West did not wear his award until after Beard and Schiff received their Silver Wolf awards in 1929. Both wore theirs and West began to wear his as well. After the Jamboree, West wrote, "I don't like the boastful atmosphere that I am afraid has crept into this report. It is true, never the less, that the Boy Scouts of America have attracted to themselves the admiring attention of scouts from all other countries."[58] In 1920 the Boy Scouts of America had more Scouts than the rest of the world combined.

At the first World Jamboree, there was a "spontaneous get to-gether" to consider a world scouting organization. The group agreed to meet again in two years. West had been reluctant to become involved, but Schiff, an international banker, thought it essential that the BSA play a part on the world stage. West took his advice. At the Paris Conference in 1922, thirty-two countries participated. The United States contingent brought home two things in use by most other Scout organizations: the left handshake and shorts as part of the uniform. West was appointed to utilize his legal skills to draw up the first constitution and by-laws for the world organization. These were approved at the 1924 conference.[59]

Scouts from the British Empire had won the Scouting competition in 1920 by displaying better pioneering, signaling, and other campcraft skills. West vowed that it would never happen again. Prior to the 1924 World Jamboree in Denmark, the BSA recruited an especially able group of Scouts. Each boy had special skills in such areas as tower building, tug-of-war, first aid, or cooking. To keep the average age under sixteen, the BSA had to find four highly qualified fourteen year-olds. Tailors made special uniforms for the contingent, and President Coolidge sent them off as representative of what was best about America. The British Scouts practiced for a week in Wembley, England before leaving for Denmark, but they did not prevail. On August 18. 1924 West sent the following telegram to Coolidge:

> YOU WILL BE HAPPY TO KNOW THAT CABLE DISPATCHES JUST RECEIVED ANNOUNCE OUR JAMBOREE TROOP HAS BEEN AWARDED WORLD CHAMPIONSHIP IN THEIR WEEKS COMPETITION WITH THIRTY NATIONS IN SCOUTING ACTIVITIES THE DANISH PRESS HIGHLY RECOMMEND SPLENDID SCOUTLIKE SPIRIT AND MANLINESS OF OUR BOYS AND INDICATE THAT YOUR WISH THAT OUR TROOP CONTRIBUTE TO THE WELL BEING RIGHT THINKING AND TRUE LIVING OF THE WHOLE WORLD HAS BEEN REMEMBERED BY OUR BOYS[60]

When the World Conference next met in Switzerland in 1926, there was apparently much grumbling about the American win and "the grave danger of competition entering into Scouting." As Chairman of the Committee on Resolutions, West was in what must have been the ambivalent position of drawing up the following resolution: "That competitions in Scouting should be minimized, and that, when they are held, they should be based absolutely and only on Scouting activities; and further, that hereafter, in connection with the great International Jamborees there be no such thing as a World Championship, but that instead, the scouts representing the various nations demonstrate their ability in self-control, yes, their ability in various activities, but not on a basis of expecting any reward, because they beat some other fellow or some other nation."[61] Perhaps the compensation for this was that it left the Boy Scouts of America as the last "world champion".

By 1929 West could magnanimously write:

> It is also characteristic of the Scout's true ideal of international felicity that he prepares for his Jamboree without any sense of rivalry with foreign nations. There are no contests. Skill and endurance are not to be matched as between the boys of 44 nations. They insist that the Jamboree is a happy get-together, not a test of ability in this or that. They are going to camp side by side, and say in effect: 'This is how we do it in our country; let's see how it's done in yours!' The Scout is a competitor only with himself.[62]

West might have evolved into an ardent internationalist or been an incredible hypocrite, but he was most likely a pragmatist who now saw a leading role for the BSA on the international scene.

Presidents and Movie Stars

West asked each incoming President of the United States to serve as Honorary President of the Boy Scouts of America. He said that it brought honor to the Scouts, which it did, but it also enabled him to interact with the President on behalf of the organization. Taft had accepted the role and did little. Wilson appreciated what the Scouts had done for the war effort and said so, but he played no other role in the Movement.

Warren G. Harding was the first President to take an active role in Scouting. His acceptance letter was upbeat: "The Boy Scouts have done a useful work, and the readiness and efficiency with which they did it, particularly during the war period, justifies our earnest hope that their usefulness may be continued and enhanced in the future. I shall be very proud to serve as Honorary President of the organization."[63] He loaned his name to the "Harding streamer," a ribbon given to 5058 troops that increased their membership by at least 25% in 1923. West was a delegate to Harding's 1922 White House Conference on Youth, but the only significant outcome was a call for vocational training for young people for the post-war economy. When Harding died suddenly on a trip to California in 1923, West mobilized Scouts to stand vigil in every station the funeral train passed on the return trip to Washington. If the train stopped, they were to present a bouquet of wild flowers to honor a "great friend."

Calvin Coolidge was equally enthusiastic about Scouting. "Both my sons are Scouts and my observation of the benefits they have derived from their affiliation has strengthened my conviction of the organization's usefulness. I shall be glad to render any proper service I can to the organization at any time."[64] Coolidge spoke at Scout gatherings and let his picture be used in recruiting literature.

Herbert Hoover's son was also a Scout. In his acceptance letter to West, he said, "In meeting the vital need that when the oncoming generation takes over our national affairs it shall be a generation bulwarked with character, the Boy Scout Movement plays a most useful part."[65] Visiting scout troops were always welcome at the White House and Hoover was happy to pose for a picture with them. Hoover convened a White House Conference on Child Health and Protection. West chaired the Section on Youth Outside Home and School. The Conference adopted a "Children's Charter" of which West was very proud.

Presidents were not the only public figures to whom West was drawn. He liked to drop names of movie stars, as well. In the May 1927 issue of *Boys' Life* he noted that while on a recent trip to Los Angeles he had had lunch with Douglas Fairbanks and Mary Pickford. In the June issue he described "Doug" as an embodiment of the motto "Be Prepared" and as a man who lived the "gospel of physical fitness." "Doug is, of course, still enthusiastically interested in Scouting and *Boys' Life* and I had to tell him about both of them. He hopes shortly to give us another article for *Boys' Life* and is casting about for that big good turn he hopes some day to do for Scouting—the making of a great scout picture."[66]

Fairbanks never produced a Scout movie but did write an article for *Boys' Life*, "If I Were Fifteen." "It is better to govern one's self by positive than by negative thoughts, to develop strength instead of bolstering up weakness, to think in terms of benefits to be gained instead of pitfalls to be avoided," he wrote.[67] West also reported that he was introduced as the Editor of *Boys' Life* to child actor Jackie Coogan. Coogan responded, "I read *Boys' Life* magazine. It is very good."[68] A cherished family photograph showed the Chief Scout Executive with Shirley Temple. He was clearly a man who knew important people. He was now an important person himself, and he had come a long way from the humiliation of the orphanage.

Program Problems

Back at the national office, many issues remained unresolved from the previous decade, and new ones emerged. A suggested move to supposedly more central Chicago was thwarted when it was determined that one-third of the Scout population lived within 200 miles of New York City. The Executive Board did establish a Supply Department office in Chicago and another in San Francisco. These were quite successful in selling axes, knives, and shoes.[69]

A new uniform was introduced in 1920 and was made mandatory on January 1, 1922. Breeches were retained for winter use, but shorts were now optional for summer wear. The high collar jacket was replaced by a shirt and neckerchief. West was very clear about the latter:

> We are anxious to have the cooperation of every Scout and Scout official in making effective the regulations covering the Official Uniform, Insignia, and Badges. To tolerate a conscious disregard for requirements, even in simple matters, breeds disrespect for law and order. When I have found boys wearing the neckerchief under instead of over the shirt collar, it develops that invariably the Scouts, and indeed their own Scoutmaster, did not understand the correct way of wearing the neckerchief. I am anxious that every Scout and Scout official study the diagram, wear the neckerchief in the *right way*, and that he invite the attention of *other fellows* to the *right way* when he finds them wearing it wrong.[70]

The entire new uniform cost ten dollars.

In 1922 West called the Girl Scouts an "imitative organization", and he was still trying to get them to change their name. He quoted from a field report that "it is just a scheme to give girls an excuse to wear bloomers and to indulge in hoydenish activities."[71] The anti-Girl Scout rhetoric cooled significantly after 1926 when Mrs. Herbert Hoover assumed the Presidency of the Girl Scouts. She was quite outspoken, and West did not want to alienate her or her husband. Mrs. Hoover wrote to a friend about a discussion she had had regarding a possible name change:

> The tone of the spokesman of the Boy Scouts was very belligerent. The President [Head] and two or three of the most active members of the Executive Committee took Mr. West's word unquestionably on this subject. At that time I talked with a number of other members of the board who are more prominent in the world - and found them all surprised that such an attitude existed with any of their officials and inclined to ridicule and even doubt the truth thereof until they made their investigations. They all felt exactly as my husband would on the subject.[72]

It seems that West had paid attention only to those who shared his views on girls and Scouting and he had not made an unbiased survey of his board.

West had better luck on other fronts in the battle of name infringement. The Excelsior Shoe Company ended the use of the word "Scout" on its coins; Winchester stopped production of its "Scout" knife and Rickenbacker Motors of its "Scout" car; the Salvation Army did not revive its "Life Saving Scouts." By the time West had stopped publishing the yearly box score in the 1930 Annual Report, 435 entities had been "dissuaded from unauthorized use of the Boy Scout name, title, insignia, and uniforms" so that "the greatest men of the nation . . . may serve without fear of commercial taint" and commercial enterprise could not benefit from an association with Scouting.[73]

One long-standing source of irritation and name confusion had been the "Lone Scouts." West resolved this by paying $8,000 for the remaining stock of merchandise of the Lone Scouts of America in 1924. This organization had been founded by William Boyce in 1915 because he felt that the Boy Scouts focused on the city and neglected rural boys. His program encouraged publication of boy-written Tribe papers and stressed individuality and boy leadership. This did not mesh well with the highly organized, adult-led model followed by the Boy Scouts of America.

The BSA had begun a program for rural boys in 1916. They were going to be called "Lone Scouts" until someone discovered that the name was already in use. West wrote:

> Now we couldn't help admiring these boys for their grit and spirit. We knew they had good scout stuff in them so we decided to work out a plan which would enable such boys to become regular scouts and allow them to wear the uniform and badges and pass their tests and have all the fun scouts enjoy.
>
> For a time we thought we would call these boys Lone Scouts. But that name didn't seem to fit very well - for we don't think they will be lonesome a bit. Then we hit upon the name Pioneer Scouts and that seemed to fit them perfectly.[74]

Pioneer Scouts wrote directly to National Headquarters for advice and instruction and had to report progress at least twice a year. The program was not promoted much until Armstrong Perry was appointed Chief Pioneer Scout in 1919. It still never had more than 1200 members.

In 1924 61,478 of Boyce's Lone Scouts merged with the Boy Scouts of America, but they retained their own advancement program, 15 Youth Councils in the United States and Canada, and 25 authorized Lone Scout publications. West assumed Boyce's title of "Chief Totem." In 1926 West wrote about the merger:

> 'Merger' is a word that has received peculiar significance in America, where men with vision have accumulated

great fortunes by bringing big business enterprises into one effective consolidation. Stockholders are benefited, while the efficiency of the unified business had been greatly heightened. The merger of the Lone Scouts with the Boy Scouts is a similar enterprise. To make the whole thing effective, both sides have to give up things to fit more effectively into each other. How effective this merger will be ultimately depends on the spirit of 'give and take' we show.[75]

This positive analogy to corporate America cast West as a captain of industry himself. He had his own product line - youth work and character development.

A year later both the Lone Scouts and the Pioneer Scouts became the Rural Scouting Division. Boyce's *Lone Scout: The White Boys Magazine* had ceased publication in 1924. The Boy Scouts of America revived *Lone Scout* in 1927. It had no subtitle and was published until 1956.

Railroad Scouting, a second program with rural emphasis, began in 1926. "One of the most unique developments in Scouting has been the precedent established by the Missouri Pacific Railroad in placing an experienced scout executive on its staff, working in the department of safety. The executive visits the small communities along the railroad lines and organizes troops of scouts. Over one hundred such troops and over two thousand scouts have been organized and the results are most satisfactory to the railroad officials. It establishes a happy relation with the people in the towns, gives to the boys a wholesome program of activities and the results are seen in part in better respect for property, fewer accidents and less depredations on the railroad."[76] Why West would then call this an "unselfish interest in the community and its social life" in the next annual report is unclear. Perhaps if business mergers were efficient, then fewer accidents and acts of vandalism were altruistic. It was a very company-friendly statement. The Missouri-Kansas-Texas, Delaware and Hudson, Southern Pacific, Chicago and North Western, Union Pacific, Milwaukee and St. Paul, and Great Northern Railroads followed the Missouri Pacific in hiring scout executives. After executives organized troops, the troops were transferred to area councils. Within a few years most of the railroad executives had transferred to councils as well, and by 1938 only the Missouri Pacific line retained one.

"The Louisville Plan"

Previously, West had not reached out to the black community, but in 1925 he wrote that, "an intensive effort can be made to strengthen and further develop work already organized among racial groups, especially colored boys."[77] The Eighteenth Annual Report for 1927 contained the first official report of the Committee on Interracial Activities. This served Negro, Indian, and foreign-born boys. Bolton Smith of Memphis, Tennessee was the first chairman. He was described as "a careful student of the question raised by the presence of the negro in this country . . . Knowing that all movements for negroes in the South were of little use unless supported by whites, he waited until the scout movement was well known and generally in use in the South before urging the extension of work among negro boys." By 1926, Negro troops under Negro leadership existed in 108 councils, but only five of them were in the South. A grant from the Laura Spellman Rockefeller Foundation provided for the hiring of black executives, so that by the end of 1927 there were black units in 167 councils including thirty-two communities in the South. Only Georgia and Mississippi did not have Negro Scouting. The next year there was at least one black unit in each Southern state.

Negro Scouting was separate but equal. "The scout movement being strictly a democracy, the committee [on interracial activities] reaffirms the position of the Boy Scouts of America in recognizing the right of every local council to determine when they will handle the situation in their own local community."[78] West was again pragmatic in dealing with the reality of a segregated nation.

Louisville, Kentucky had the most black Scout troops in the South (twenty-six) and the organizational scheme there became known as the "Louisville Plan."

> The activities of the colored department parallel those of the white but are kept strictly separate. Practically all of the colored troops are connected with colored churches and all are under colored leadership. Training courses for colored leaders are conducted at frequent intervals and every prospective leader is required to undergo training before entering upon his duties. A Colored

> Court of Honor passes upon the qualifications of all candidates for advancement, meeting monthly for this purpose.

> Care is taken to avoid any possible clash between white and colored scouts. No distinction of any kind is made in designation of troops, wearing of uniforms, and other insignia or in any other scouting material. Joint activities, however, are studiously avoided. An attempt is made to give the colored scouts equal privileges with the white. The colored boys have their own rallies, field days, and other special activities. Each year a separate camp is maintained for colored scouts and leaders.[79]

Councils with a number of black troops had separate summer camps. Otherwise, black Scouts would attend the same camp after the white boys had left but the camp would often then operate under a different name.

A Colored Advisory Board reported to a committee of the Council Executive Board but had no member on the parent board. There was a separate office in the colored district. This was summarized as "a parallel but distinctive organization, equal in privileges but with no joint activities."[80]

It would still be ten years before the last southern council (Delta in Mississippi) accepted Negro Scouting in principle. That did not mean that these councils actually enrolled any black scouts at that time. Segregation and discrimination were not limited to the South. In 1929 Chicago's Owasippe Scout Camp had a separate colored camp as did many other northern councils. Executives at the 1928 Biennial Conference refused to support a resolution by one of the three Field Executives for Negro Boys that Negro Scoutmasters who could not read be able to earn the new Scouter's Training Award by having the material read to them. To his credit, West had supported the resolution.[81] He voted for quality program rather than prejudice.

Resistance to Negro Scouting was compounded by the white face of Scouting literature. The first picture of a black Scout did not appear in *Boys' Life* until 1926 and they were rare after that. Then, there were the jokes in the "Think and Grin" section. In December 1927

West wrote: "We believe that jokes with a double meaning, or with a questionable meaning, or with a suggestive meaning, should be strictly taboo among scouts, and absolutely ruled out of Scout publications of every kind."[82] "Questionable meaning" was apparently limited to sexual innuendo and did not apply to "darky" jokes. There were many, but one will suffice: "Parson Jonson, you hadn't oughter swiped dat chicken 'cause de debbil set it just to tempt you, he did. Jonson Well, suh, den de debbil sho' los' his chicken."[83] Black Scouts were probably also not thrilled with the 1924 pressing of the first official Boy Scout phonograph record, "Ole Zip Coon." Little wonder that black boys did not rush to become Scouts.

Other Concerns

In addition to enrolling more Scouts from under-represented groups, West was concerned about "membership leaks." Scouts dropped out. West continued to believe that the lack of older boys in the program was the result of the failure of leaders to present the program properly, not a problem with the program itself. "It is also a general feeling that the scout program has in itself the necessary elements to hold the interest of the older boy."[84] Some superficial changes were made. In 1926 the position of Junior Assistant Scoutmaster was created for 15 year-olds (the Senior Patrol Leader position had been created in 1919), and in 1927, palms were added for earning merit badges beyond those required for Eagle rank. In theory, these changes created positions of greater responsibility for older boys and gave them incentives to stay in the troop.

Very limited changes were made to accommodate those with handicaps. On September 15, 1923 an "Achievement Badge" was approved with alternate requirements for Second and First Class ranks if a Scout were "crippled or suffering from physical disability." No exceptions were allowed for merit badge requirements and, consequently, for higher ranks. In 1918, West had said:

> It would be a great mistake for us to have the first class badge mean an acceptance by us of a standard of young manhood which recognized physical disability or inability in any degree. As you know, I went all through

this as a young man on crutches and I appreciate the other side of the story very keenly. Frankly, I believe that the Scout Movement will do greater good for the greater number of boys by having the first class badge mean that a boy is physically fit. Indeed, I would favor a more rigid requirement in this particular, because we are all more keenly alive to the importance of physical fitness in the program of preparedness, and Scouting must join with other agencies in setting a high standard in this direction.[85]

By 1923, he welcomed the Achievement Badge: "I have been keenly interested in this development of the subject because I myself, as a boy, could not have qualified as a first class scout on account of a physical disability which made it impossible for me to get around without the aid of crutches. I can fully appreciate what many splendid fellows have felt and I am very happy now that they will be given this opportunity."[86]

West might consider limited alternatives, but he never compromised about standards. "We differ from other attempts to do organized work for boys in that we maintain standards. Our insignia for tenderfoot, second class, and first class scouts and our various merit badges are awarded under very carefully safeguarded conditions. This helps in maintaining the respect and active interest of boys and is an important element in our own success in establishing the Movement on a permanent basis."[87] He believed that he produced a high-quality product, and he wanted to exercise quality control.

West applied the same rigorous standards to leadership methodology. As the Boy Scouts of America continued to be adult-centered, the European Scouting organizations embraced the concept of boy leadership of patrols. They also camped by those smaller units rather than in the large institutional camps favored by the BSA. In the United States, in the 1920s, only Scoutmasters, not Patrol Leaders, could sign off on advancement requirements. Around 1925 a young Dane named William Hillcourt came to work at the national office. According to Hillcourt, he met West on the elevator one day and West, in his characteristic fashion, asked the young man what he thought of the organization. Hillcourt had been a Scout in his native Denmark, corresponded with his Danish patrol members as long as he lived, and was never accused of being shy. He spoke up and told West that the BSA needed more focus on the patrol method where boys learned together from a boy leader. West asked him to prepare a proposal, and Hillcourt submitted a draft of the first patrol leaders' handbook. This was published in 1929 and Hillcourt took the patrol leader's emblem, two green bars, as part of his identity, "Green Bar Bill," as he became a writer and regular contributor to *Boys' Life*.[88] West demonstrated his lack of understanding of the boy-led patrol, the heart of the patrol method, as he compared the patrol to a neighborhood gang. "You have, through the patrol system, an opportunity to have just the kind of gang we wished for [when we were boys ourselves] and in addition you have something we never even hoped for—men to help."[89] It seemed to West that it took adults to keep the program mission-focused, but he did accept the concept of boy leadership and always respected Hillcourt for speaking up.

Camping was considered a vital part of Scouting whether by patrol or troop. Scouting Magazine noted:

> Annually the boy scout in whom race instincts are not ground out by civilization, returns to the ancestral home in the woods. Camp means to him better oxygen for his lungs, but a stretching of the lungs to their full capacity. It means the matching of his wits with the new environment. It means fellowship of a new kind with many boys and with a few men. It means the testing of his soul by rain and discomfort and the many quiet inward victories that make for character.[90]

By 1928 32% of Scouts went to summer camp. West encouraged troop activities in city or town for troops that did not go to summer camp. Year-round camping was still in development. For West, camp was another opportunity to provide an "attractive, practical, worth-while program [that] may be used to help the boy spiritually and morally."[91] Camping also required adult leadership, was mission-focused, and, incidently, could be fun.

The program evolved very slowly with such very small changes in advancement, the patrol method, and camping. West had to be convinced that change was necessary and worthwhile before change could take place.

Boy Adventurers

The Reading Program Committee and the Publicity Committee joined forces in the promotion of Scout adventurers. Books by boys about their adventures were quite popular and the committees thought that such experiences might highlight the great character developing aspects of Scouting.

The March 1928 issue of *Boys' Life* contained a notice: "How Would You Like to Go to Africa?"[92] The proposed trip was a summer safari with Osa and Martin Johnson to photograph animals in British East Africa. Scouts applied through their local councils each of which chose one candidate based on outdoor experience and ability to write. Two hundred candidates were reduced to the seven who were interviewed by West, Col. Roosevelt, and George Palmer Putnam, explorer and sponsor of the trip. Three Eagle Scouts were chosen. After being outfitted at the Boy Scout Trading Post in New York City and "a night in Mr. West's beautiful home," they boarded a ship for Africa. They wrote about their adventure in *Three Boy Scouts in Africa* and in his introduction, Martin Johnson said of them that they had "left a fine impression of the real American boy."[93]

A greater adventure, however, started with the July 1928 *Boys' Life* notice "Do You Want to Go with Byrd to the Antarctic?"[94] Cdr. Byrd wrote, "I have always been a warm friend of the Boy Scouts and a firm believer in the value of its training . . . I am happy that circumstances make it possible for me to include a representative chosen by the Boy Scouts of America in this expedition. I look for great things from my Boy Scout. Health, loyalty, youth, and ambition mean a great deal in exploration, and the Antarctic is the greatest challenge left in exploration today."[95]

Applications were forwarded to the national office where selection was based on outdoor skills, leadership ability, and writing talent. Six Scouts were chosen to come to New York City to be interviewed by West, his committee, the 16th National Training School, and Commander Byrd. Paul Siple (rhymes with disciple) was selected. An Eagle Scout with sixty merit badges and Sea Scout experience, Siple was a biology major at Allegheny College in Pennsylvania. He boarded his ship in August 1928, and Scouts at home eagerly awaited each issue of *Boys' Life* to follow his progress.[96] Siple so impressed Byrd over the fourteen-month experience that he was invited to head the Biology

Department on Byrd's second Antarctic expedition in 1934.

Siple wrote three books, *A Boy Scout With Byrd, Exploring at Home,* and *Scout to Explorer.* He also spoke frequently to Scout groups and service clubs about his experiences. He was unfailingly positive about Scouting. For example, in a 1931 address he said, "It [Scouting] furnished a program so interesting that it filled all my spare moments completely, and there was no time to be tempted by all the side steps that could have been taken at that time in my life." He mentioned the skills he had learned while earning merit badges and while sailing with his Sea Scout Ship on Lake Erie. "In many ways, altogether too numerous to mention, Scouting has aided me and will continue to aid me, and the only way in which I will ever be able to repay Scouting for the great debt which I owe it, will be in the service and the hope of instilling in other boys the inspiration Scouting has meant to me."[97] West took great pride in Siple and his achievements and pointed out repeatedly that he represented all 600,000 Scouts from whom he had been chosen to serve, not just the 88 who had applied. (Siple was to make a total of six trips to Antarctica and in 1956 chose another Eagle Scout, Richard Lee Chappell, to accompany him.)

Two less dramatic adventures also occurred during the summer of 1928. Eight Chicago Sea Scouts manned the schooner *Northern Light* on a cruise on the Borden-Field Museum Arctic Expedition. The four Eagle Scouts who had been finalists but not selected to go to Africa with the Johnsons drove the Lincoln Highway from coast to coast in a covered wagon (actually a converted Reo Roadster.) They publicized the highway and promoted highway safety with demonstrations at each stop. They recruited a patrol in each town to set up markers simultaneously when the Expedition reached San Francisco.[98] West noted that: "These opportunities were offered to Scouts because Scouts have received training that qualifies them to take part in this sort of adventure. These expeditions required of their members moral character, physical fitness, experience in camping and outdoor activities, resourcefulness, courage. No ordinary boy could qualify. Boy Scouts were gladly accepted because they have learned to 'Be Prepared.'"[99]

Honors

In 1926 the Executive Board authorized the Silver Buffalo Award. This award was intended to honor those individuals who had made significant contributions to Scouting at the national level and was modeled on Baden-Powell's Silver Wolf in Britain. The order of presentation of the Silver Buffalo awards was West's chance to formalize the history of Scouting in accordance with his Historical Statement. The first award went to Baden-Powell, the second to the Unknown Scout, and the third to William D. Boyce "who brought the Movement to America." The path continued with presentation of the fourth Silver Buffalo to Colin Livingstone who was present at the incorporation and the first president of the Executive Board. The fifth was awarded posthumously to James J. Storrow, the second board president. Beard and Seton were sixth and seventh respectively, and Robinson was eighth. The ever polite and deferential Robinson later wrote, "I do not think the Boy Scouts movement at large, either in England or America realize how much they owe to the YMCA for helping them get started." This comment was in response to a letter from William Murray when he was writing the history of the BSA. Murray had written: "if I felt free to designate the real Father of the Movement in America, I would put in your name, but of course this would not be wise."[100] For those involved, it was not inclusion that mattered but the order of precedence. Beard, Seton, and Robinson all believed that their awards should have come earlier in the sequence.

West received the twenty-first and Fisher the twenty-second of the twenty-two Silver Buffaloes awarded by the National Court of Honor that first year. West's citation read: "James E. West, lawyer, identified with the organization of the Playground Movement, Juvenile Court of Washington, national Child Rescue League, Secretary of the Roosevelt White House Conference on the Care of Dependent Children, Chief Scout Executive of the Boy Scouts of America since January 1st, 1911."[101]

West chose two other occasions to reiterate and embellish his "cherished tradition" by which Scouting came to America. On July 4, 1926 the Silver Buffalo was presented to the Unknown Scout in the form of a Bronze Buffalo statue at Gilwell Park in England. In describing this presentation in *Boys' Life*, West called the Unknown Scout a

"Pathfinder" because "he could find his way in a fog, and to call the fog of London thick is to describe it very mildly. Literally, you cannot see your hand before your face. The street lamps become just pinheads of light when they do not disappear altogether. It might just as well be midnight on the darkest night in the country."[102] West was consistent in his presentation of events when he delivered the eulogy at Boyce's funeral in Ottawa, Illinois on June 13, 1929. "To the foresight and generosity of our beloved William D. Boyce we owe the origin and full development of the American Boy Scout movement, one of the most forceful elements in the building of our young manhood."[103]

A seemingly trivial matter that grew to have major consequences was the design of the Silver Buffalo award itself. West proposed a silver buffalo designed by A. Phimister Proctor and suspended from a red and white ribbon worn around the neck. Beard wrote, "I very much prefer the braided horsehair. It will give more distinction to the wearer, be more suggestive of red blood and masculine qualities than a ribbon which any boarding school girl might have tied around her pretty neck."[104] West's opposition to horsehair caused Beard to complain to Frederick Vreeland, one of his supporters on the National Court of Honor. "Ours is a big machine, a tremendous machine and the biggest men of the nation are only too glad to be named among us, therein lies our strength and therein lies our weakness. It is a centralized machine and that gives tremendous power to people who should not have it, but what is the answer, I am listening?"[105] Vreeland replied: "The only answer I know is to put a soul in the machine. If you can't do it, I don't know who can."[106] Beard was unable to change the machine as West remained firmly at the controls. The red and white ribbon remained, and the machine retooled Beard's National Court of Honor.

On June 17, 1927 the Executive Board changed the makeup of the National Court of Honor to a body of "purely judiciary character." Judges replaced Beard's "expert advisors on merit badge subjects." One of those who was replaced was Vreeland, the radio advisor. He was incensed and joined Beard in his condemnation of West whom he thought responsible for the change. The decision had been made by letter ballot of the board. Vreeland complained to board president Head that, "the opinions of the members are subject to review by the office staff, and the Chief Scout Executive becomes in fact the censor as well as the canvasser of their ballots. His power in such matters is extremely great."[107]

Vreeland had written requirements for the Radio merit badge. They were impossible for boys to meet. Vreeland also objected to Second Class Scouts earning merit badges. "What a boy wants is a hard task he considers worthwhile." To Head he complained: "You have put into the hands of one man very great powers, amounting practically to a dictatorship. Are you sure this man will use these powers to continue Scouting as a great moral and molding force: helping to make men real, virile men the type of men the country needs, or will he make it a machine for the quantity production of boy scouts. The situation is critical."[108] Vreeland chose to frame the argument in terms of West rather than in terms of his work on the Court of Honor which was equally at issue. Beard readily supported Vreeland:

> The Executive Board is composed of business men and the thing is conducted as would be a big banking concern, a big manufacturing concern or a big business corporation of any kind. The members of the Executive Board are a splendid lot of men. They are kind-hearted, conscientious men but awfully busy men; consequently, everything is put into the Executive's hands with the result that the Executive is more powerful than the Board itself. The Executive today practically owns the Boy Scouts of America.[109]

Beard did not consider Vreeland's impossible requirements, but joined him in his criticism of West.

Vreeland concluded, "I am weary of this perpetual struggle trying to persuade Mr. West to play the game according to the rules. He does not seem capable of doing it," and "of course the whole thing is unconstitutional, but what is a constitution between friends."[110] Beard remained as Chairman of the National Court of Honor for the rest of his long life but he was left with a purely symbolic role. Vreeland was not reappointed to a national committee and he never received the Silver Buffalo for his earlier work. West remained firmly in control of the machine.

End of a Decade

On December 27, 1927 the Boy Scouts of America moved to new headquarters at 2 Park Avenue. There only West and Fisher had private offices. Everyone else sat at long rows of desks, by Division, the epitome of bureaucratic organization. At the time of the move, the national office staff had grown to 321 employees. West himself had two secretaries, E. H. Vitalius and T. J. Murphy. Both were men. "No smoking was allowed nor could any man be seen in shirtsleeves. Every afternoon, he [West] toured the office, straightening window blinds, questioning employees, perhaps sweeping a desk clean with his cane if it looked cluttered."[111] He had been doing this for years, and no one apparently objected publicly to his behavior.

Even though there were no behavioral changes at the national office, there were some administrative changes. In 1927 the Executive Board created the Personnel Service. With mandatory training of new professionals, the annual executive drop out rate had been reduced from twenty-seven percent in 1919 to twenty percent in 1927. The new Personnel Service was to analyze and address the reasons for why the turnover was still so high. The solution for retaining executives followed the same pattern as the solution for retaining boys - more training in the same program. Introduced in 1926, "The Scout Executives' Growth Program" stressed experience, training, reading, writing, and community service. It provided recognition for men who met the standards. Executives were encouraged to recruit and train more volunteers to extend their influence and lighten their loads. District Commissioners, Assistant District Commissioners, and Neighborhood Commissioners would provide direct service to the troops, and District Committees would provide training, advancement review, and activities. Executives would oversee their work.

The Department of Education authorized some colleges to conduct credit courses in Scouting education (90 in 1929) and others to provide non-credit training in conjunction with local councils (185 in 1929).[112] With more training, the Scout leaders at all levels would be able to do their jobs better, have greater job satisfaction, and remain in the program longer.

George Ehler, Assistant to the Chief Scout Executive, compiled reams of statistical charts to profile training and every other aspect of the Movement. He also kept the "Red Flag List," a confidential file of "names of men who are found to be unfit for leadership in the Boy Scout Movement."[113] West was clear that his goal was not to retain everyone. Criteria for inclusion in the confidential file were not publicized, but financial misconduct, rather than what would now be considered issues of morality, was apparently the most common reason.

In 1929 the National Executive Board also decided that all volunteers had to register and pay a fee. While promoted as part of the streamlined administrative process, the fee also helped balance the budget. Fisher explained: "Everyone should by some specific act definitely subscribe to the Scout Oath and Law, sign an application blank and become an avowed member of the entire Movement and have in return a membership card which he will carry as a reminder, just as does the Scout. A membership fee seals the act, makes definite the commitment which otherwise might be done carelessly and superficially.

"It is essential that all who are related to the Movement feel deeply the full meaning of the Scout program. There should be pride in belonging, a sacred feeling of obligation, a joy in assuming responsibility. We believe the registration adds to this sense of crusadership and comradeship."[114] West followed up by saying that "to look upon the registration fee as a tax or assessment is to miss the spiritual significance of the procedure. A membership fee seals the act, makes definite the commitment which otherwise might be done carelessly and superficially."[115] West spoke as if paying dues were a sacred act and a moral obligation. He did not feel the same about other issues that had not arisen from his desk.

In 1928 the Executive Board of the Cleveland Council responded to a billboard that promoted smoking by girls by passing a resolution that "Scouts would approach women smoking in public, asking them to give up the habit" as they felt that "smoking by women coarsens them and detracts from the ideal of fine motherhood."[116] The National Council responded: "It is not within the province of the Local Council, or even the National Council, to undertake to pass resolutions or legislate on any one of the many problems before the American people. We are obligated by our Constitution and By-Laws to avoid participation in controversial and political questions."[117]

The response was followed by a national press release: "Any such activity as boys approaching women with an urge to stop smoking was emphatically disapproved by the National Scout Authority . . . Mr. West pointed out that the Boy Scout Movement seeks to instill habits of good character in boys but it does not intend to lead Boy Scouts to interfere in the private and personal concerns of adults."[118] This did not apply to Scout leaders. West had previously wished "that the day may come when the Boy Scouts of America, with their ideals of leadership, will impose upon themselves a sufficient restraint to make it unthinkable for a man to be a leader of boys and find it necessary to puff incessantly on a cigarette." He called them "coffin nails." Democracy had its limits. This was an example of West's pragmatic approach in conflict with his administrative model. He supported local council standards in such areas as racial segregation, but not in areas where he and the national office had established specific guidelines. A local council could not refuse to collect fees or pay its quota. It could not deviate from advancement requirements nor could it authorize Scouts to participate in purely political events. West considered the anti-smoking campaign to be political and he did not want Scouts to take part in it.

If the anti-smoking campaign had been framed as educational and not been directed solely at women, then it might have been perceived differently. The Chief Scout Executive frequently referred to his character building work in terms of education. He often referred to the BSA as the "world's greatest educational agency." At the Fourth International Boys' Work Conference in Chicago, he said, "We are trying very hard to keep in mind that our interest is in boy life, that our interest is in producing a trained citizenship for the nation, men of character trained for the responsibilities of citizenship, rather than the mere creating and perpetuating of an organization."[119] West considered himself to be an altruistic educator.

In 1928, West received an honorary LLD from Kalamazoo College. The citation read, "Scholar, attorney at law, expert in public welfare, conserver of childhood and youth, humanist in law, and inspirer of American citizenry." The same year he also received a Master of Humanics degree from Springfield College as "one of the founders and promoters of a great movement among the boyhood of this and other lands."[120] West preferred the doctorate and made it clear that he was to be called "Dr. West." He was an important man and should have an important title as well as the respect due that title. The orphan had come a long way.

When Dr. John Finley, former President of the University of the State of New York, introduced West at the Biennial Conference later that year, he highlighted the honorary doctorate. "I like to think of him as the Doctor of Light and Leading. [a play on LLD] With that interpretation I salute him. But I think we must take a great deal of credit to ourselves for his degree. It is *our* degree. We have educated Mr. West all through these years. He had very little training when he came to us and now he has won the degree which I think belongs to us, and in so presenting him I do so with a particular satisfaction that he has brought that honor to the Boy Scouts of America. I present to you Dr. James E. West."[121] West did not respond to Finley's remarks other than to say "thank you." He then went on to introduce the guests in the audience. West had difficulty in responding to personal observations and preferred to remain in his professional role.

One executive noted that, after 1929: "West expected official uniform, a left hand handshake, no smoking, and to be called 'Dr. West.' My first introduction to the man was at a Region 1 Conference. I was wearing unofficial long pants, a Stetson wide-brim hat, held a cigarette in my left hand, and said 'Nice to meet you Mr. West.' Is it any wonder I stayed in Rhode Island my whole career?"[122] There were standards that professional Scouters had to meet and West modeled them. He always wore the official uniform to Scouting functions and he smoked his cigars only in the privacy of his home or clubs.

Standards for Executive appearance extended to the office as well. West expressed distress "because of the lack of appreciation of some of our men as to the importance of having the right kind of office in which to work; not necessarily an extravagantly furnished office, but an office which is so equipped and so located as to be in keeping with the position which an Executive holds, and to put the Scout Movement in that relationship to the community which its importance deserves."[123] With and without impressive offices, The Boy Scouts of America had a net membership of 842,540 at the end of the decade (December 31, 1929). It had been an impressive decade of growth in membership and in the development of the professional corps that guided that membership.

Notes

[1] Beard Library of Conngress (LOC) 130 6/12/16

[2] Proceedings of the 5th National Training Conference (NTC) 1928, page 246

[3] Phillips, John. "Selling America: The Boy Scouts of America in the Progressive Era, 1910-1921." Unpublished Master's thesis, University of Maine, 2001

[4] West, J. "Stumbling into citizenship." BSA, 1920 page 3

[5] Eleventh Annual Report of the BSA page 9

[6] Tenth Annual Report of the BSA page 36

[7] *Community Boy Leadership.* BSA, 1921. Page 238

[8] Ibid

[9] See Malatzky, D. *Summer Camp!* New York: Greater New York Councils, 2002

[10] *Boys' Life* 11/33 page 44

[11] Murray, W. *The History of the Boy Scouts of America.* New York: BSA, 1937, page 267

[12] *Scouting* 10/10/19 page 3

[13] *Scouting* 8-9/60 page 10

[14] *Scouting* 10/10/19 page 3

[15] Pote, Harold. *Fifty Years of Scouting in America and the Pioneers.* Printed privately, undated, page 19

[16] Murray, page 276

[17] *Community Boy Leadership.* Page 572

[18] *Scout Executive.* 5/20

[19] *Community Boy Leadership.* Page 19 underlined in original

[20] Ibid page 21

[21] Ibid page 24

[22] Ibid page 179

[23] Ibid page 83

[24] Ibid page 162

[25] Ibid page 34

[26] *Scout Executive* 5/27 page 8

[27] Proceedings of 2nd National Training Conference (NTC) 1922 page 119

[28] Ibid page 252

[29] *Scout Executive* 3/23 page 2

[30] *Scouting* 5/27 page 65

[31] *Boys' Life* 10/23 page 32

[32] *Boys' Life* 11/34 page 3

[33] Beard LOC 129 2/02/14

[34] Beard LOC 212 1914

[35] Mcleod, David. *Building Character in the American Boy.* Madison: University of Wisconsin Press, 1983 page 158

[36] Murray, page 82

[37] Pote, page 16

[38] Sixth Annual Report of the BSA page 4

[39] *Scout Executive* 11/23 page 6

[40] Colin Livingstone was President from 1910 to 1925. James Storrow from Boston assumed the Presidency in 1925 but died ten months later. Milton McRae, his Vice President completed the term but did not seek re-election. Walter Head, an Omaha banker, took over in 1926.

[41] Beard LOC 132 1/15/26

[42] Beard LOC 131 5/07/21

[43] Crump, I. "Thirty years of service to others." *Boys' Life* 1/41 page 16

[44] R. Tait McKenzie was a Philadelphia surgeon and sculptor who created the statuette in 1915. For models, he used five different boys to fashion his "ideal Scout."

[45] Beard LOC 131 6/30/23

[46] Beard LOC 212 6/04/25

[47] Beard LOC 4/21/24

[48] Quoted by Salomon, J. *Three Great Scouts and a Lady.* Unpublished manuscript, 1976 page 237

[49] *Boys' Life* 6/29 page 202

[50] *Boys' Life* 8/26 page 25

[51] Helen West, personal communication

[52] Ibid

[53] Beard LOC 132 12/08/26

[54] Beard LOC 132 12/23/26

[55] Proceedings of 6th NTC 1936 page 53

[56] Don Green, personal communication

[57] Monroe, Keith. "Jim West: Scouting's Gruff Genius." *Scouting* 11-12/74 page 8

[58] *Boys' Life* 10/20 page 51

[59] Lund, Richard, *The Boy Scout International Bureau.* Unpublished manuscript, 1971

[60] Beard LOC 131 8/18/24

[61] Proceedings of 4th NTC 1926 page 298

[62] *Boys' Life* 3/29 page 24

[63] *Boys' Life* 5/21 page 2

[64] *Boys' Life* 10/23 page 5

[65] *Boys' Life* 7/29 page 24

[66] *Boys' Life* 6/27 page 60

[67] *Boys' Life* 4/29 page 7

[68] *Boys' Life* 6/27 page 60

[69] Beard LOC 131 3/25/22

[70] "Scouting with a neckerchief" BSA 1927. Italics in original

[71] Beard LOC 131 3/25/22

[72] Salomon page 170

[73] Proceedings of 3rd NTC 1924 page 325

[75] *Scouting* 8/01/16 page 1

[75] *Boys' Life* 2/26 page 32

[76] Seventeenth Annual Report of the BSA page 79

[77] Sixteenth Annual Report of the BSA page 17

[78] Eighteenth Annual Report of the BSA page 89

[79] *Scouting* 10/24 page 5

[80] Ibid

[81] Proceedings of 5th NTC 1928 page 104

[82] *Boys' Life* 12/27 page 13

[83] *Boys' Life* 1/19 page 26

[84] Sixteenth Annual Report of the BSA page 16

[85] *Scouting* 8/1/18 page 13

[86] *Boys' Life* 11/23 page 26

[87] 1916 speech in West archives at Springfield College

[88] Bill Hillcourt, personal communication

[89] *Boys' Life* 2/26 page 45

[90] *Scouting* 3/11/20 page 3

[91] *Boys' Life* 6/28 page 5

[92] *Boys' Life* 3/28 page 43

[93] Douglas, R., Martin, D. & Oliver, D. *Three Boy Scouts in Africa.* New York: G. P. Putnam's Sons, 1928 page xiv

[94] *Boys' Life* 7/28 page 9

[95] *Boys' Life* 9/28 page 11

[96] Walter Ardini, personal communication

[97] *Boys' Life* 4/31 page 26

[98] *Boys' Life* 8/28 page 25

[99] *Scout Executive* 10/29 page 3

[100] Edgar M. Robinson Archives at Springfield College 2/04/35

[101] *Boys' Life* 6/26 page 46

[102] *Boys' Life* 9/26 page 20

[103] Petterchak, J. *Lone Scout: W.D. Boyce and American Boy Scouting.* Legacy Press, 2003 page 273

[104] Beard LOC 132 3/24/26

[105] Beard LOC 132 4/20/26

[106] Beard LOC 132 4/21/26

[107] Beard LOC 125 8/13/27

[108] Ibid

[109] Beard LOC 125 11/04/27

[110] Beard LOC 126 undated

[111] Monroe, page 8

[112] Twentieth Annual Report of the BSA page 148 ff

[113] *Scouting* 3/23 page 2

[114] *Scout Executive* 8/29 page 1

[115] *Scouting* 11/29 page 350

[116] *Boys' Life* 9/28 page 6

[117] Ibid

[118] Beard LOC 133 7/14/28

[119] Beard LOC 133 11/28/27

[120] *Boys' Life* 7/28 page 4

[121] Proceedings of the 5th NTC 1928 page 29

[122] H. C. Anthony, personal communication

[123] Proceedings of the 5th NTC 1928 page 353

WILLIAM D. BOYCE
1858 - 1929

DANIEL CARTER BEARD
1850 - 1941

ERNEST THOMPSON SETON
1860 - 1946

JAMES E. WEST
1876 - 1948

Baden-Powell and Dr. James E. West at Schiff Scout Reservation (circa 1934). Photograph taken by Bill Hillcourt.

Left: Albert Rose portrait
of Dr. West - 1935.

Below: Scout Day at the
1939 World's Fair.

Above: Franklin D. Roosevelt, Dr. West and Dan Beard during the Presidential Review at the 1937 National Scout Jamboree.

Left: James E. West in his frock coat (circa 1914).

Above: Dr. West being interviewed by Lowell Thomas at the 1937 National Scout Jamboree.

Right: The editor of Boys' Life at his desk.

Left: West family Christmas card (circa 1920).

Below: 1939 West family Christmas card.

Back Row (*Left to Right*): Arthur, Marion, and Bob.

Front Row: (*Left to Right*): Jane (*Mrs. Arthur*), Dr. West, Lynn, Mrs. West, Helen.

Dr. West standing, Hubert Martin, First Secretary of the International Committee, Dan Beard, and Walter Head, President of the BSA, at the 1926 Executive Conference.

Dr. West, Dan Beard, and Col. Theodore Roosevelt in 1937.

Patch worn by Dr. West as Chief Scout.

The Chief Scout Executive.

JAMES E.
1876 — 1948
BOY SCOUTS OF AMERICA
1911 — 1948

James E. West's gravesite in Kensico Cemetery Valhalla, New York.

Chapter 6

The Thirties

The Great Depression produced hard times for Scouting as it did for the rest of the country. Cash flow was so bad that the national staff had to take a cut in pay. The hard times in conjunction with overgenerous estimates of the number of potential new Scouts led to West's greatest failure, the Ten Year Recruiting Program. His greatest triumph was delayed for two years by a polio epidemic, but the Twenty-fifth Anniversary/First National Jamboree did finally become a reality. If West could not control local recruiting or polio, then he compensated by tightening control over the organization itself. He also experienced recurrent health problems but his will to overcome them did not have the power that it had had in his youth. Some things did not change. Beard continued to complain, and the Girl Scouts still refused to change their name.

The Numbers Game

In March 1930 President Herbert Hoover kicked off a ten million dollar endowment campaign for the National Council, Boy Scouts of America. As originally conceived, three million would cover accrued liability and start the Retirement Fund, one million would be working capital and establish a national training center, and six million would form an endowment to reduce the need for annual campaigns. The campaign was suspended in June after only three million dollars were raised. Some of that had been pledged as matching gifts and was written off, so that, in the end, only 1.6 million dollars were raised. The national staff was reduced in number and the remaining staff first took a ten percent pay cut in 1932 and then an additional five percent cut in 1933. Uniform prices were reduced in 1931 and the price of *Boys' Life* was cut from twenty cents to ten cents in October 1932. West wrote: "We shall be ready to discard as an organization requirement any item of routine procedure involving time or expense which cannot be justified in the light of our two outstanding fundamental responsibilities: First to create and maintain conditions so that boys intensely desire to be scouts; second, to create and maintain conditions so that men are willing to give service."[1] West was pragmatic enough to adjust to bad economic times.

Despite the shaky finances, membership continued to grow. West and the Executive Board believed that in hard times the country needed Scouting more than ever. He wrote Baden-Powell that "undoubtedly, the nation-wide program of service activities has captured the imagination of not only the Scouts and Scout leaders, but of the general public who has contributed a great deal to stabilizing our government." He also predicted that the year 1931 would close without a deficit.[2] (There was a surplus of $3850 in a budget of nearly one million dollars.)

In 1932, the Ten Year Recruiting Program began with great fanfare. West wrote: "The Ten-Year Program is the Scouting Program, lifted to a planned basis of creating, or influencing character in sufficient number of the boyhood population of America as to produce a citizenship of such force in numbers and virility in action, as to materially influence the life of our Nation." West continued that this was not a recruiting effort but a "great civic crusade" to build character and to make "one of every four new male citizens a four year Scout trained man."[3] Significantly, this slogan of "one of every four" did not apply to the Negro race.[4] Each unit was to set a goal for increased membership and recognition in the form of flagpole plaques was provided to troops that met their goals. Although there was a modest membership growth each year, it was never on the scale to reach "one of every four." Mention of the Ten-Year Program in the Scout literature disappeared by 1936, although troops that met their recruiting goals continued to earn annual awards through 1941.

Anniversary

In 1931 West celebrated twenty years as Chief Scout Executive, and Walter Head, President of General American Life Insurance Company, completed his fifth year as President of the Boy Scouts of America. He wrote to West:

> My close personal relationship with you as the Chief Scout Executive presented me with an opportunity to know you and to know you well and, at the same time, determine for myself the measure of efficiency which is injected into the Boy Scout movement by your driving force and personality . . . While, at times, there has been disagreement and, in a few instances, conflicting opinions have been held by us, yet in the main, I respect and admire your ability and sincerity in successfully dealing with the great problems which both the volunteer and the employed officer is seeking to solve.[5]

In a similar vein, Lord Hampton wrote:

> James E. West was a wonderful companion throughout my tour . . . West has built up an intensive system of organization but has contrived that this shall not obscure real Scouting. He is a fluent and forceful speaker and rightly puts efficiency before everything else in his dealings with a large staff. My impression is that he gets both efficiency and loyalty in return.[6]

Both men spoke of West's amazing ability to get things done. He drove himself and expected the same drive from those who worked for him. He was obviously respected by those workers who stayed on the job. There are no published figures about staff turnover at National Headquarters, but those who were inefficient or disloyal obviously did not stay.

Mortimer Schiff had been waiting impatiently for Head to step down as Board President, but Schiff had a problem. As West wrote to Baden-Powell, "Obviously there are some problems involved, but what a fine testimonial it will be to the power of Scouting to have a Jew elected as the head of a great Movement here in America."[7]

Schiff was, in fact, elected President, but he died suddenly after only one month in office. Head was elected to complete that term and he stayed on as President for the rest of West's tenure as Chief Scout Executive. In his will, Schiff left one hundred thousand dollars to the Boy Scouts of America and ten thousand to West personally "in token of my appreciation of his faithful and self-sacrificing service on behalf of the boys of the United States." Fisher also received ten thousand dollars.[8] In 1932 Schiff's mother bought a four hundred acre New Jersey estate called "Brookrace" and gave the BSA a quarter of a million dollars to establish and endow a memorial to her son. The Schiff Scout Reservation in Mendham, New Jersey was officially dedicated as the national training center on October 18, 1933. In his dedication, West wrote, "May it become an inspiration and of practical service to the Scout Movement here in America for generations to come." All professional training courses and most volunteer programs were then offered at Schiff.

A Sick Man

West was not well physically. Tuberculosis had crippled him as a child. The disease had lain dormant in his body and reappeared as an intestinal ailment. In September 1931 he wrote to Beard, "I have not fully recovered. It may be necessary for me to go to the Mayo Clinic at Rochester for a check-up and possibly an operation. I had the benefit of the best medical treatment abroad and feel that I am being wisely advised here."[9] On September 26, he wrote from the hospital, "I am glad to be able to write to you personally and say how grateful I am to you and the many friends in New York for all their expressions of friendship. After all, what is there more precious in life than evidence of friendship?" He noted that his fever was down and that he was undergoing tests to see "if the germ which has caused all the trouble can be located any place else in my body."[10] On October 7 he added "Sometime when the opportunity presents, I shall be glad to tell you something of the very difficult experience through which I have gone."[11]

By April 1932 West was doing well enough that the National Council passed the following resolution at the Annual Meeting:

> Resolved, that the National Council extend to James
> E. West, Chief Scout Executive, their congratulations
> upon the encouraging signs of improvement in his

health following his recent illness. They urge upon him
the necessity for continued precaution in order that
we may continue to have the benefit of his leadership
unimpaired.

They express appreciation for his good judgment, his
basic understanding of the fundamentals of work for
boys, his organizing ability and his vigorous leadership
to which in large measure the success of the Boy Scouts
of America is to be attributed. He is an outstanding
figure in social work and owing to his broad interests
and contacts the program of Scouting has been enriched
by cooperation with other organizations such as the
White House Conference on Child Welfare where his
leadership has been exceptional. The National Council
reaffirm their confidence and express the hope that
they may have the benefits of his leadership for many
years to come.[12]

In 1931 Mrs. West had surgery for a goiter and in 1932 Arthur
was also ill. "Certainly the ever jolly and happy Mrs. West has had her
share of tragedy and trouble in life, but I feel and believe that relief is
just ahead."[13]

In February 1933 West and his wife were guests of Dr. John Harvey
Kellogg at the Miami Springs Branch of the Battle Creek Sanitarium.
West described this to Beard as a "very unusual experience." Kellogg's
"unusual" regimen included not only morning cornflakes but also a daily
enema and sexual abstinence.[14] Because of or in spite of the treatment,
West improved. Beard wrote to West: "I want to congratulate you upon
your healthful appearance, also upon your ability and will power which
enables you to return your initial vigor and enthusiasm. I think you have
many reasons for feeling happy."[15]

Because of his illness, West was unable to travel extensively. In 1933
he gave Beard $150 per month from his travel budget, and, in 1934,
$4800 from the surplus. Beard stopped complaining about "Green Bar
Bill" Hillcourt's increasing role as the expert on outdoor activities and
the patrol method, long enough to write West: "Let me congratulate
you upon the perfection of the organization and the masterly manner

in which it is being managed."[16]   Only a cynic could believe this had nothing to do with money received.

West also delegated much to his Deputy Chief Scout Executive, George Fisher. "During the last few years, since my health has made it necessary for me to sort of be a privileged character, from the standpoint of regular attendance, Dr. Fisher has just done everything, not only to make me feel that I shouldn't strain myself but also to carry on. We all owe him a great deal."[17]   Fisher spent most of his time in New York City when West was ill. His first published job description in the 1932 Annual Report was a bit mysterious. "The Deputy Chief Scout Executive has a wide range of activities and relations, many of which are of such an intimate nature in matters of counsel with individuals, services, and divisions, that they can not be recorded in a report of this nature."[18]   This was a masterly way of saying that he promoted harmony at headquarters by getting West to see other perspectives on issues of concern to him and by smoothing the feathers that West ruffled on a regular basis.

The West family was doing well as indicated in a letter to Beard in 1934. Arthur had graduated from Cornell in June and was headed to Yale Law School. "Marion goes into her Junior year at Mount Holyoke College, Helen, we hope, will enter Vassar, Bob will enter Lawrenceville, Exeter, or Andover."   Bob chose Exeter, perhaps because Arthur had attended Andover. The girls had gone to high school in New Rochelle. All family members were again in good health.

The Depression / Franklin D. Roosevelt

For West and the Boy Scouts of America, the Depression was both a challenge and an opportunity. "Relatively speaking the Boy Scouts of America has not suffered greatly. In certain sections of the country there have been reductions in budget and in personnel, but generally speaking, there is evidence of determination on the part of the community to maintain the standards of scouting in the face of all obstacles."[19]   West believed "depression service approximates war service." "By showing a spirit of cheerfulness and willingness, the boyhood of America can do a great deal to upbuild the morale of other people. By doing this they will not only accomplish a great deal of good but also secure for themselves a summer of enriched happiness and worthwhile activities.

Let us SMILE and DO, and perhaps in this way we can inspire others to SMILE and DO and thus create a positive force for good throughout the country."[20]

Scouts gave service indirectly by serving as messengers and by aiding social service and relief agencies. They helped directly as they collected, handled, and distributed clothing, food, toys, and literature, especially as a "Christmas Good Turn." Service furthered the mission of the Boy Scouts of America, but the publicity didn't hurt either. "In all these plans we should be conscious of the *character values* that are given to the boy in being of service. As never before we should seek opportunities which will be for the good of the boy, as well as the Scout Movement, and to dramatize the educational values of our service as a character-building organization. Efforts should be made to have as many boys in uniform in community service as possible."[21] West was again pragmatic and advertised his product. He encouraged high profile public service as the best way to improve the positive image of Scouting in America.

The opportunities for service increased dramatically after Franklin D. Roosevelt was elected President of the United States. Roosevelt was the first President to have been an active Scouter. He had chaired the first Greater New York Committee on Scouting in 1920 and organized the Boy Scout Foundation of Greater New York in 1922. He paid off the $50,000 debt which the New York City Scouts had accrued, and financed a council in each borough of the City. He was the force behind the purchase of Ten Mile River, the twelve thousand acre Greater New York Council camp. Roosevelt received the Silver Buffalo award in 1930 when he was still Governor of New York. The award was presented at camp. In his acceptance, Roosevelt said: "The Scout Movement provides the boy with a real program of activity which challenges his interest as such. It not only builds the interest, it builds character, the basis for citizenship. That, just now, seems the more important. It is the solution of the crime problem through prevention, rather than correction."[22] An Honor Guard of Eagle Scouts served at his inauguration in 1933.

With notices in *Boys' Life*, West mobilized Scouts across the country to listen to the President's radio broadcast on Saturday, February 10, 1934 at noon EST. Roosevelt challenged them to collect household items for those in need. As he would then do for the next several years after Roosevelt spoke to the Scouts on Anniversary Week, the Chief Scout Executive asked all Scouts who were listening to raise their right hands in the Scout sign and repeat the Scout Oath with him. Over the next eighteen days, the Scouts collected a great deal of material for distribution by the Federal Relief Administration. The 496 participating councils did not keep records in the same way so that the total collection was reported as, "1,182, 284 items plus 225 truckloads, 134 tons, 329 pounds, 820 boxes, 1,448 bags, 93 bundles, 12 bales, 88 sets, 1 warehouse-full, 5 houses completely refurnished, $91.29 in cash and $2,354.38 worth of food."[23] Roosevelt later asked the Scouts to distribute and collect pledge cards and literature supporting the National Recovery Administration's "Buy Now" week.

In the summer of 1933, Roosevelt made a speech at Ten Mile River:

> This spring because of my Scout training, I took a leaf out of the notebook of Scouting in order to take care of a lot of boys who are a bit older than you are—boys who had graduated from high school and some of them from college, but who had not been able to get work for a year or two or three years.

> And we started in this country, modeling it to a large extent after Scouting, a Civilian Conservation Corps, and today there are two or three hundred thousand older boys in various parts of this country in these civilian conservation corps, taking care of forests, preventing fires, stopping soil erosion, and doing a thousand other tasks that the country needs.

> And I am told that in these camps of course, when you get a camp of 200,000 boys together some of them naturally develop into leaders and I am told that the boys who have had Scout training are coming forward more rapidly than any others and are becoming the leaders of a great many of these civilian conservation camps.

> It is a pretty fine tribute to what Scouting has done
> throughout the country.[24]

Scout leaders conducted training for recreation leaders in Civilian Conservation Corps (CCC) camps and provided merit badge training, handicraft, entertainment, and literature for those in the Corps. The CCC is often considered to be one of the major accomplishments of the New Deal and the BSA was proud to serve as a model and to support it.

Rigidity

Throughout his tenure as Chief Scout Executive, West believed that the Boy Scout program would attract boys between 12 and 15 and would maintain their interest if it were properly utilized. He did acknowledge that boys dropped out of the program. "The real solution to our tenure problem will not come through tricks and devices. The Scout Program now has the basis for maintaining the interest of boys year after year, when it is conducted properly. There is no magic way to success in this respect. We succeed only as we understand the facts and know how to use them. If we are to succeed in holding a sufficient number of boys to four years' tenure it will be due to the fact that we have created a type of Troop leadership that knows how to administer the Scout Program properly."[25] He did not believe that either a "younger boy problem" or an "older boy problem" existed and he saw no need to develop different programs for them.

West believed that boys younger than 12 should not be Scouts. Baden-Powell had started the "Wolf Cub" program in England, in 1916. B-P's program was based on Rudyard Kipling's *Jungle Book* in which a wolf pack adopts and raises a young boy named Mowgli. The wolf would become the universal symbol of Cubbing as the fleur-de-lis was the universal symbol of Scouting. Wolf Cubs did many Scout-like outdoor activities, and West did not believe that these would be appropriate for American boys.

Emerson Brooks had organized The Boy Rangers of America in Montclair, New Jersey in 1914 and "in 1918 at the suggestion of Mr. James E. West, Chief Executive of the Boy Scouts, the Rangers were incorporated in New York State without expense to our organization."[26]

The Boy Rangers were 8 to 12, wore middy blouses and shorts, and followed an Indian theme. Their Constitution was the twelve points of the Scout Law, and they looked like a Scout organization except that women could serve as "Guides." "The Chief Guide prefers efficient women to inefficient men."[27] Both Chief Guide Brooks and his Assistant were active Boy Scout Commissioners in Montclair. Ranger National Headquarters was one block from BSA headquarters in New York City. Mark Jones had suggested that the Boy Rangers be integrated into the BSA but West disagreed. He thought that a program for younger boys would discourage them from becoming Scouts when they reached age twelve. He believed that his executives and volunteers had enough to do with Boy Scouts and, beside that, there were no women in his program.

In introducing Emerson Brooks at the 1924 Biennial Conference, West noted that in response to a perceived need for a program for younger boys, Brooks had "worked out something entirely different and gave it an entirely different name. It has worked under conditions which divorced it in the mind of the boy and the parent and the community from any relationship to the Scout Movement. I thought that a fine thing, then, and I hope you will agree with me."[28] At that time the Boy Rangers had 88 Lodges and 8,000 members. West's younger son Bob was a Boy Ranger although West complained in a 1926 letter to Beard that when he accompanied his son on a Boy Ranger sponsored family trip up the Hudson River, it "lacked proper adult leadership."[29]

In 1925 West finally asked the Laura Spellman Rockefeller Foundation for a grant to study the "younger boy problem" in the United States. He had written to Schiff that he had asked psychologist and educator H. W. Hurt "to determine the kind of program which will be most serviceable to boys under 12 years of age and less likely to wear out their interest in Scouting. My own hope is that we can develop something that will strengthen interest in home life and stimulate the influence of fathers and mothers and sisters and brothers in home activity and home recreation, and avoid a program which will infringe upon the peculiarities of the Scout Program."[30]

West also believed that there would be limits to such a program. "It will be made available where the record of the local council activities shows that the leadership in that community is available to take on this added responsibility without handicap to the Scouting Program."[31]

He thought it premature to endorse any organization for younger boys, but the Boy Rangers were "probably the best of the lot" and already met his criteria. "Every effort is made to prevent encroachment on the programs of the Scouts or other organizations for older boys, in order that should the graduate Rangers eventually join any of them, nothing which they have learned in the Ranger organization shall prevent their perfect enjoyment of the new programs furnished."[32] Despite the prohibition, at least one Council (Iowa City, Iowa) used the Ranger program and one (Aberdeen, Washington) imported the Wolf Cub program from Canada.[33] The Honolulu, Hawaii Council used the British program.

An experimental younger Scout program began in 1929. The American program was quite different from the British one as it was home-based, and would not preview Scout skills and activities. Hurt had recommended that women could serve as Cubmasters as they did in England and the Boy Rangers, but this was not to be. Women could only serve as Den Mothers under the supervision of a male Cubmaster. In Scouting they could counsel a boy in merit badge requirements but only a man could sign off on them because of the importance of the "boy-man relationship in character development."[34] West also insisted that the boys be called "Cubs" and not "Cub Scouts." His sentiments were articulated by New England Executive Ralph Nodine: "One of the principles upon which Cubbing is based is the differentiation from Scouting in the boy's mind. The Cub must not feel that he is a 'junior Boy Scout.'

'Cub Scouts' is a term used by some Councils. This immediately associates the Cub with Scouting in the mind of the boy himself and in the minds of the public. Our literature calls the boys 'Cubs,' which avoids all association with Scouting. Therefore, let them be 'Cubs,' and not 'Cub Scouts.'"[35]

Beard had previously written to Schiff to object that "Cub" was "too English and demeaning to frontiersmen and Indians." He wanted the younger boys called "Buddies."[36] Four years later, he insisted to West that he had originated the word "Cub" and their two- finger salute.[37] All restrictions as to which councils could use the experimental program were finally lifted, and Cubs became a regular part of the Movement in 1933. The Boy Rangers disappeared. Although 8000 Den Mothers were active in 1936, they were not registered in the program and literally did not count as members.

There were problems with "older boys," that is, those over fifteen, as well. At the National Council meeting in 1930, Dr. James Russell, Dean Emeritus at Teachers College, Columbia University, had lectured that even the schools were losing their grip on 14 to 15 year-olds and that Scouting would need a genius to find an appealing program for older boys. West neither understood nor accepted this view. He believed that he already had the program and simply needed the right people to deliver it correctly. He said that "Senior Scouting" was "an extension of the program of the troop with new avenues of adventure and new appeal" that would carry the Scout's interest until his twenty-first birthday.[38]

In addition to Senior Scouts within troops, there were two other Scout programs for older boys. Sea Scouts had been around since 1912 and existed in three-quarters of the local councils. Their focus was educational rather than vocational, as it was in England. "Rovering," an individual program for Scouts over eighteen became official in 1933 but was never promoted by West and the national office. The 1939 Annual Report stated that "it [Rovering] is not being aggressively promoted because it is felt that the greatest need, and therefore the greatest emphasis at the present time is for program material for young men between the ages of 15 and 18." The British program had a Knights of the Roundtable theme that did not appeal to many in America. Rover membership peaked at 2271 in 1939 but had dropped to 824 at the end of World War II, and the program stopped accepting new members in 1947.

These were not the only programs that failed to find a place in West's heart or in the Scouting program. E. Urner Goodman founded The Order of the Arrow in Philadelphia in 1915 and H. Roe Bartle founded the Tribe of Mik-O-Say in St, Joseph, Missouri in 1925. Bartle brought Mik-O-Say with him when he was transferred to Kansas City in 1928. Both were honor societies based in Boy Scout summer camps and many other councils had similar groups. Goodman and Bartle were both close to West, but he never allowed either man to promote his program nationally. As early as 1922 he had warned, "I don't need to tell this group what the spirit of Scouting is. Go ahead and run your organization in your own camps, but don't try to push the expansion. Let it grow, if it will, on its own merits and not through a promotional effort on your own part."[39] As an "official program experiment" the

Order of the Arrow had grown enough to become an acceptable local council activity in only sixty-eight local Councils by 1936. West became an "honorary" member in the Siwanoy Council in 1938. Mik-O-Say never grew beyond the two councils.

Woodbadge, a training course for adults, began at Gilwell Park in England in 1919. In 1936 Col. J. S. Wilson from Gilwell ran experimental courses in Rovering and Scouting at Schiff Scout Reservation, and Bill Hillcourt served on the staff as Wilson's assistant. West attended part of the training but the national office (West) later determined that the course was "too British" and "wouldn't work here." Hillcourt was not asked to revise Woodbadge to make it more American and the course did not reappear in the United States until long after West had retired. It is interesting to note that Goodman, Bartle, and Hillcourt were all dynamic individuals and West may not have wanted competing personalities and hierarchies within his organization. These activities were not his idea and they represented diversions from the program as he envisioned it.

Boys' Life

As Editor of *Boys' Life* after 1923, West had an outlet to expound upon his vision of youth development. His editorials covered a wide range of topics but they could be reliably found to emphasize a few favorite themes such as the Scout Oath, motherhood, an annual physical examination, the Daily Good Turn, summer camp, and God. His points were clear, concise, and inspirational:

> I have taken advantage of every opportunity to make clear that, in my judgment, physical fitness is a primary obligation, and to stress the importance of every individual's feeling personal accountability for his own health, by finding out what his condition is, and taking effective measures to correct remedial physical deficits and make and keep himself physically fit.[40]

> * * *

> Are you mentally awake? Have you become a slave to routine and tradition, or have you developed the ability to think things through for yourself? Do you

have an inquiring mind? Do you accept what is said to you without analysis? Do you organize your mind and thinking so as to go on mental explorations? Is each new day an adventure for you? . . . With many there is confusion between mental alertness which is the ability to think things through, and scholastic attainment in school. While high marks very often reflect hard work and intense application, they do not necessarily indicate that one is mentally alert.[41]

* * *

Young man, I believe this. I think there is nothing more important than giving a boy or girl religious instruction as a foundation for life, giving it under conditions where they personally feel it and accept it and respond to it and put it into practice. Take every opportunity that comes to build your foundations strong and sturdy so that you may not only get peace and happiness yourself in life, but be in a position where you can serve your fellow men and serve God.[42]

* * *

The boy who lets his tired mother pick up his clothes for him instead of hanging them up neatly, who has to be called several times in the morning before he will get up, who neglects to weed the garden or to make some little repair around the house, is a slacker. What a fine thing it would be if every boy made up his mind to take a real share in the responsibilities of his home![43]

West reported on national meetings as if the Scouts might be interested. "Say, you would have enjoyed seeing the thoroughness with which these boy-minded men discussed Scouting. It was stimulating to see the type of men who are working for our Movement."[44] West may have thought that boys might identify with these men as he, himself, did or he might have been pointing out that boys and men were part of the same Scouting community. Regardless of his motivation, the subject was not appealing.

To stimulate Scout participation in *Boys' Life*, West offered an 8" x

10" autographed photograph of himself for the three best reports (under 100 words) of Troop Good Turns printed each month. He continued to publish Good Turn reports, but very few contained a Scout's byline. At the same time, a Scout could win a Scout diary if a joke he submitted were printed in the "Think and Grin" column. The diary was apparently more popular than the picture.

Consultation

West believed "a boy is quite like a bicycle stable when going somewhere,"[45] and he had to provide the momentum. He also believed that he considered the boy's point of view:

> In every given question that I have to share in the responsibility of deciding, I first subconsciously, and more often definitely, look at the McKenzie Boy Scout statuette on my desk or in some other way get into my mind a picture of a boy and then endeavor to think through the problem with basis of how it will best be solved for him, rather than what is the most convenient thing, or even the most expedient thing to do from an organization point of view. It sometimes makes my course more difficult to give major consideration to the boy point of view but I believe that in the long run this has done more to help my administration of the Boy Scout Movement than any other single factor.[46]

West's definition of "a boy's point of view" was what was best for the boy from West's perspective. It seems unlikely that a boy would have agreed that picking up his clothes, weeding the garden, attending Sunday School, or eating a balanced diet were priorities.

The Chief Scout Executive also believed that he was open to suggestions. "I am always very anxious to have someone in Scouting regardless of in what capacity he may serve, feel that it is his privilege to give suggestions and to ask for help in clearing up any misgivings that he may have in any phase of Scouting, or present recommendations on any subject which he feels will lead to a better understanding of Scouting and more productive efforts."[47] Again, this was West's perspective. Only the bold and self-assured made suggestions to West. He did accept some from Fisher and Hillcourt and probably from others as well.

West did not appreciate some suggestions. On June 21, 1934 West fired George Porter, Director, Division of Business. Porter had suggested to Executive Board members that West was micromanaging: "The division has had no tools to work with except that of complete dominance by the Chief Scout Executive."[48] Porter also thought that *Boys' Life* should be sold as Mark Jones had recommended. The magazine was losing money and Porter believed that West wanted it to continue only because one-third of his $24,000 salary came as Editor, which he was "in name only." Porter had been one of West's four original division heads, so he probably approached West before complaining to the Board. If West rejected a suggestion, there was no appeal.

Lindbergh

West admired men of "strong moral principles." He especially liked Charles A. Lindbergh. Thirty-three and one half hours after taking off from Curtiss Field on Long Island, New York, Lindbergh landed his *Spirit of St. Louis* at Le Bourget Airport outside Paris on May 21, 1927. This first non-stop, solo flight across the Atlantic made "Lucky Lindy" an international hero. West sent him a cable on behalf of the BSA: "The congratulations of 840,000 scouts on your achievement so splendidly typifying the spirit of American youth."[49]

Lindbergh had never been a Boy Scout although he once said that he had studied for his Tenderfoot tests, but the family moved and he never joined a troop. West deeply admired Lindbergh for his "good clean life, self-discipline, and preparedness."[50] Lindbergh had mastered mechanics, marksmanship, and science as a boy, and West characterized those experiences as equivalent to Lone Scouting. West and his editorial assistant Peter Lamb wrote *Lone Scout of the Sky* as a tribute to that image.

In July 1927 the Executive Board elected Lindbergh the eighteenth Honorary Scout. The citation read, in part: "Your splendid record of courage and confidence based upon thorough preparation, and the qualities of character you have since manifested so thoroughly harmonize with what we desire to have set before the boyhood of America as an ideal, that we are greatly pleased to confer upon you this honor."[51] Eagle Scout James Campbell delivered the citation to Lindbergh and was warmly received. Lindbergh later wrote, "I think that of all the honors I have been fortunate enough to acquire, the election as an Honorary Scout is the most prized by me. I am so thoroughly in sympathy with the aims and activities of the Scouts."[52] Lindbergh's interest in Scouting seemed to relate to aviation: "Boy Scouts of today will be the flyers and engineers of tomorrow. The Scout program gives the Boy Scout who is anxious to prepare for a career in aviation an opportunity to master many of the details of an aviator's position. Signaling, compass reading and mapping are invaluable in aviation."[53] West agreed with Lindbergh's goal "to make boys air-minded." He also wanted to secure Lindbergh's celebrity endorsement of the Scout program.

West and Lamb collected the writings of Honorary Scouts in another book, *Boys' Book of True Adventure*. Lindbergh had written a series of in-flight notes for the *New York Times*. Lamb edited those notes as Lindbergh's contribution to the Scout book. Lindbergh also entered Scouting's pantheon of "boy's hero-immortals" on the cover of the new 1927 edition of the *Boy Scout Handbook*. Norman Rockwell was asked to replace Davy Crockett in the original sketch with Lindbergh in the final one. In 1931, another book by West and Lamb, *The Boys' Book of Honor*, again emphasized Lindberg's virtue and character.

When Lindbergh and the *Spirit of St. Louis* undertook a three-month, eighty-two city tour of the United States, Scouts were prominent at every stop. They marched in parades, served as honor guards and color guards, and assisted in crowd control. Scouts were one of the few groups that the shy Lindbergh seemed comfortable in meeting and this pleased West. Lindbergh followed his North American tour with a sixteen-country Latin American visit. This tour became the subject for the cover story in the March 1928 issue of *Boys' Life* and the 1928 *Boy Scout Yearbook*.

In 1928 Lindbergh was awarded the Silver Buffalo. The citation read: "Col. Charles A. Lindbergh, aviator, world hero, ambassador of American good will to Europe and Latin America. His courage and achievements have captured the imagination of the boyhood of the country; his modesty, poise and qualities of sterling character, his exemplification of the Scout Motto, 'Be Prepared,' have set them a standard of worthy conduct; his devotion to the cause of aviation has challenged them to an ideal of Service. The inspiration of his whole record is outstanding today in its service to boy life."[54] Lindbergh was invited to the national meeting that year to receive his award but he could not attend. In 1931 West reported that Lindbergh had visited the national office and that "formal presentation of the Silver Buffalo to him will be made some time in the near future.[55] Lindbergh was invited to the annual meeting each year through 1935 but he rarely accepted invitations to such public events and the Scouts were not an exception. Apparently he never received the decoration, as it is not among his 131 national and international honors in the archives of the Missouri Historical Society. West wanted to make a public presentation, and Lindbergh did not oblige.

On the day after the Lindbergh baby was kidnapped on March 1, 1932, West sent a telegram to each council urging them to mobilize all Scouts in the country for the search. He asked them "to be alert and watchful and cooperative in every way possible in seeking clues or information as to the Lindbergh baby."[56]

Finally tired of all the publicity about the kidnapping, the baby's death, and the trial of the kidnapper, the Lindberghs moved to Europe in 1935 and did not return until 1939. While in Europe, Lindbergh was asked to assess the military aviation capability of Germany. He was impressed. In 1938 he received the Service Cross of the German Eagle from Herman Goering on behalf of Hitler for "services to world aviation." Lindbergh was firm in his belief that the United States should not intervene in a European war and that a strong Germany would serve as a buffer against Soviet expansion. Like Pope Pius XII, he could never bring himself to denounce Nazi social policy and genocide. After his return to the United States, Lindbergh became a spokesman for America First, a group that embraced American neutrality, as had Lindbergh's father, a five-term Congressman from Minnesota before World War I. Unfortunately for Lindbergh, he became identified with some very anti-Semitic supporters and Nazi sympathizers, and instead of being America's hero he was seen by many as America's traitor. This certainly did not mesh with the image that West was trying to create. Lindbergh's name did not appear as a member of the National Council or as an Aviation merit badge advisor in the 1940 BSA Annual Report. The 1940 printing of the *Boy Scout Handbook* had a new Rockwell cover, and the internal reference to Lindbergh's "good manners" was eliminated.

Although Lindbergh redeemed himself to some degree with the general public by his role as a civilian "technical advisor" to the Air Corps and by flying fifty combat missions in the Pacific, the Boy Scouts of America never again embraced him.

Author

In addition to *Lone Scout of the Sky*, *Boys' Book of True Adventure*, and *Boys' Book of Honor*, West wrote, co-wrote, or edited three other books. *He Who Sees In The Dark* was a biography of the American and British Scout Frederick Burnham with whom Baden-Powell had spent a few hours in Africa. West might have used the opportunity to suggest that Burnham, and not Seton or Beard, was the American who had taught Baden-Powell all he knew about "Scouting." Instead, he followed Burnham's autobiography, *Scouting on Two Continents*, closely and did not make that claim. These four books were co-written with Peter Lamb. Lamb had been West's editorial assistant and Assistant Editor of *Boys' Life* from 1923 to 1929 and was an independent writer after that. He had been gassed during World War I, was never in good health, and died in 1935.

William Hillcourt was the co-author of *The Scout Jamboree*, an account of the American contingent's trip to the 1933 World Jamboree in Hungary. The only book that West wrote by himself, *Making the Most of Yourself*, a collection of his *Boys' Life* editorials, was published in 1941.

Silver Anniversary

During his first annual National Good Turn radio broadcast from the White House during Boy Scout Anniversary Week on February 10, 1934, President Franklin Roosevelt, Honorary President of the BSA, extended an invitation to all Scouts in America to come to Washington, DC in August 1935 for a unique celebration of the Silver Jubilee of the Boy Scouts of America, a Jamboree. In April, West went to San Francisco to meet Baden-Powell who was on his way home from Australia.[57] Baden-Powell said he would try to return for the Jamboree.

The National Jamboree Committee chaired by President Head based its plans for the 30,000 Scout encampment on the four previous World Jamborees. The site was completed and many delegations were enroute on August 8 when President Roosevelt "announced with very deep regret the necessity of canceling plans for the Boy Scout Jamboree in Washington, August 21 to 30 . . . The President was advised by the Surgeon General, Commissioner Allen [of the District of Columbia] and Dr. West that the decision reached by the conferees was based upon the prevalence of poliomyelitis in two epidemic centers in Virginia, within about 100 miles of the District of Columbia, and the increased prevalence in other sections of the country. While the prevalence is not considered to be unduly alarming, the conferees decided it would be in the best interest of the Scouts and all concerned to cancel the Jamboree."[58] "Creative alternatives" had to be arranged for troops on the way or already on site in Washington. The BSA had taken out a $400,000 "loss of use" policy and received a settlement of $250,000 so that all registration fees were refunded to the Scouts. It has been suggested that far fewer Scouts than anticipated actually registered for the Jamboree and it was cancelled to avoid bankruptcy rather than a polio epidemic. The actual number of refunds was never published. On October 17, 1935 the Jamboree was rescheduled for 1937.

January 2, 1936 was West's Twenty-fifth Anniversary as Chief Scout Executive. Characteristically enough, it began with a whiny letter from Beard:

> Sorry that an oversight on your part deprived me of the pleasure of congratulating you on your Silver Jubilee of which I read in this morning's *Times*. Possibly your cup of joy was so full that my congratulations were not necessary to add to your happiness on the anniversary day. Be that as it may, it adds to my pleasure to send my sincere, though belated, congratulations to you and to the office force, for the splendid and efficient manner in which you have conducted the business of Scouting.[59]

The Executive Board commissioned a portrait of West by Albert A. Rose. The smile in the painting was a figment of Rose's imagination. There are many photographs of West, and they rarely show him smiling. One copy of the portrait was hung at Schiff Scout Reservation, and a second was presented to West on January 8. At the portrait presentation, Mrs. West received a Tiffany vase and twenty-five American Beauty roses. This was not the only painting that West had. Norman

Rockwell had painted the Boy Scout calendar for Brown and Bigelow since 1925. Brown and Bigelow retained the rights to the images, but the Scouts had the paintings. Four of these found their way home with West and all appeared to have special significance for him. "A Scout is Reverent" (1940) reminded him of the Law he had added and which he found to be the most important. This painting hung in his office at home where he could see it from his desk. "A Scout is Helpful" (1941) originally showed a rumpled Scout rescuing a girl from a flood. West objected to that image and insisted that Rockwell redo it with the Scout in a perfectly pressed uniform. Rockwell also calmed the flood and put a kitten on the Scout's shoulder. Despite this episode, Rockwell would later say of West that "he was always kind and considerate and friendly to me."[60] "A Scout is Loyal" (1932) reminded West of the virtue he most appreciated, and his son Bob was the model for the fourth painting, "A Good Scout" (1935).[61]

West appeared modest about the Silver Jubilee. "I am a wee bit afraid that some of the statements made in the letters and in the press over-emphasize the part that I have individually had. It has been a team game. Many individuals have been important factors in contributing to the outstanding success of Scouting here in America."[62] The history of the BSA by William Murray deliberately repeated the multiple contributor theme and downplayed West's role. Mark Jones would have been pleased if he actually believed it. West later wrote to Admiral Byrd, "I feel as a humble laborer in the ranks trying as best I can to carry on in developing fundamental qualities in boys. It is my conviction that most of the negative factors in life are based upon selfishness and greed and lack of opportunity for understanding the customs and beliefs of others."[63] West was the driving force behind the success of Scouting, and he knew it. His protestations of humility, while sincere, must have seemed hollow to those who knew him well.

As part of Deputy Chief Scout Executive Fisher's dinner tribute to West, he said, "His was the example of one completely possessed by the cause in which he was engaged: a profound immersion in the Scouting task, a rare ability to keep in touch with the minutia of the Movement, to read innumerable reports and get their meaning." As part of his speech, Fisher mentioned Ralph Waldo Trine for the first time. West once acknowledged that he had read everything that Trine had ever written. Trine was an early proponent of the power of positive thinking. As an introduction to *In Tune With The Infinite* in 1908 he wrote, "Within yourself lies the cause of whatever enters into your life. To come into the full realization of your own awakened inner powers, is to be able to condition you life in exact accord with what you would have it."[64] West believed. West responded to Fisher, "No man controls it [the Movement,] although I am fearful that this pugnacious, aggressive disposition, as Dr. Fisher has so charitably pointed out, does give evidence sometimes to some people that woe be unto the fellow who crosses my path! Actually I am the most timid soul in the world. (laughter)"[65] The laughter said it all.

The Chief Scout Executive was not at all timid when it came to defining his program and its potential for change:

> I am sometimes asked if it is my belief that it will be necessary to change the program of Scouting to suit our changing social order, and how much? I do not know how anybody can answer that question except on the basis of giving an opinion. I venture to give this opinion for what it is worth. I doubt if the time will ever come, when the need for a program of leisure time for boys and girls will be any different from what it is today. I do not believe that the time will ever come when there will not be a need for agencies to help stem the tide of evil influences and hazards to youth inherent in the changes already inherent in social life. I go further and state that I do not believe the time will ever come when the fundamentals of the program of Scouting will change. There will always be need for a leisure time program to supplement the home, the church, and the school for building character and training for citizenship.[66]

West was quite dogmatic in describing the fundamentals as he saw them. Among the elements were the outdoor program, the uniform, and reading:

> If we are to justify Scouting as an outdoor movement we must further promote camping as an organized Scout group activity. A young man, looking back on his

experience as a Scout, should have had the opportunity to get out with nature - into the open - the woods, where he was able to make his own camp, to do his own job and stand on his own two feet.[67]

* * *

The Scout uniform is a part of the romance of Scouting. It is a symbol of the ideals and outdoor activities for which the Movement stands. It has the picturesque touch which helps the Scout identify himself with the great traditions of our outdoorsmen - the pioneer, explorer, scout, and cowboy - which underlie the psychology of Scouting.[68]

* * *

Reading is an essential factoring the leisure time of almost all boys, and wholesome reading does in a very definite and practic al fashion supplement the idealisms of the program of Scouting.[69]

After twenty-five years, that now famous 1909 fog was getting even worse for Boyce with each retelling: "All day long the great city of London had been in the hard grip of a dense, heavy fog. Traffic crept cautiously and slowly. Street lights had been ordered on by the police before noon, and night was now coming on. Danger lurked on every hand."[70]

Most of West's ideas had not changed after twenty-five years, but he did mellow a bit about guns. He agreed to be an Honorary Director of the International Air Rifle League which promoted a Father-and-Son Air Rifle Contest to "encourage this real sport." In deference to West's own history, boys without fathers could also compete.

At the opening ceremony of the Sixth National Training Conference for Scout Executives held at French Lick, Indiana from March 1-18, 1936, J. Harold Williams from Rhode Island made a presentation to West:

For twenty-five years you have told this organization what to do. There are a good many men here in this audience tonight who have grown up in Scouting with you . . . There are men here who have been bawled out by you (laughter). There are men here who have been praised by you (laughter). And, Dr. West, there are times when men have been afraid of you in this Movement, afraid of you, with that tremendous energy and vitality, afraid of you with that determination to get to the end of things (laughter), afraid of you with that evidence of boundless enthusiasm, and yet, Uncle Jimmy (laughter and applause), there isn't a man who has been in Scouting long but has learned to respect you as a square-shooter, and a fair and honest American citizen.

We have been inspired by your two great slogans: 'What are the facts?' and 'What is best for the boy?' but, Uncle Jimmy, I want to go a step further tonight. All of these men here want to love you. They want to have real affection for you. There isn't a man here but wants to be your friend and wants you to be personally his friend. Honest, sir, we would like not to have to call you Dr. West; we would just like to call you Chief or Uncle Jim. And sir, these men with all this love and affection in their hearts, want to do something for you on your birthday party.[71]

They gave him a new Ford Sedan which cost $716.50.

West then replied. "I do, of course, greatly appreciate this testimonial . . . As I analyze the situation myself, when the suggestion is made that I go a little soft here and there - well, I do not know how to do other than as I think is the true and right way to do, and if course that does mean that sometimes you hit your head against things and stub your toes. Well, that is part of life."[72]

Later in the conference West made an interesting observation about himself but directed it at the other executives:

I do venture to emphasize the references made in the last part of the report to the obligation of one to take care of one's self and I speak from a very vivid personal experience. There was one time in my life when I was very happy in the realization as to what I could 'take,' what I could do. Now I find it takes more strength of character and will power to do the sensible thing, and I am finding some satisfaction in the ability to rest and build up. I want to recommend that idea to you men who rather pride yourselves on the lateness with which you can carry on your - well, we will call it discussions - whatever they may be, those of you who pride yourselves on what you can eat, regardless of the hour, and other tests of endurance. In reality, you are breaking down your own effectiveness as a leader, and, certainly, you are setting a very poor example.[73]

Although Beard was unable to attend the conference, he found other things to complain about. After a traveling French Scout visited the national office and he was not invited to meet him, Beard wrote to West: "Did it not occur to you that it would be the natural thing and the courteous thing to have given that little French Scout an opportunity to meet the National Scout Commissioner. Courtesy is worthwhile."[74] Beard also continued to fret about the order of his Silver Buffalo ten years after the presentation. West replied:

It still remains a fact that it was the sixth award made. I wish I could do something to change this, but after all, is it a matter of such great importance? There is only one Dan Beard and regardless of who is before him or who comes after him, nothing in history is ever going to change his place in what actually has happened in the development of the Boy Scouts of America. I just wish you did have enough confidence in the rest of us to fight your battles for you in matters of this type. Your one sole job now should be to keep well and healthy and get out of life all of the satisfaction to which you are entitled.[75]

In recalling his speech at Beard's eighty-fifth birthday party, West wrote, "I spoke of the love and affection in which Dan Beard is held by everyone in the Scout Movement from its highest officials to the newest incoming Tenderfoot."[76] West needed Beard and tried to keep him happy, but he also seemed to genuinely like the man. After twenty-five years of interaction, both must have seen it as a well-choreographed dance.

Since 1919 Beard had led the Annual Pilgrimage to the grave of Theodore Roosevelt in Oyster Bay, New York. West always supported it. "While I have purposely kept in the background, I have nevertheless been very appreciative of the values and given every possible support to the program each year, and it is a pleasure for me to do so again this year."[77] Beard characteristically responded that "the accumulative success of the affair is largely due to the generous assistance and lack of interference by the organization."[78] The dance continued.

A Christmas card from the President capped the year for West:

> The White House
> Washington, D.C.
>
> To the Boy Scouts of America:
>
> Yours has been a worthy record upon the pages of which are written courage, dependability, faith, loyalty, and service. You have won a signal place in the life of the youth of America. As today you are the Boy Scouts of America, so with years to come may you be the men to whom your country can look for the realization of unselfish devotion and civic righteousness. I wish you all a Merry Christmas.
>
> Franklin D. Roosevelt[79]

Jamborees

The first National Jamboree was finally held in Washington, D.C. from June 30 to July 9, 1937, and it was a personal triumph for West. He organized it, promoted it, and did it without federal money. The whole operation was a tribute to his skills. Lorne Barkley, Director of Program, observed that "every detail in the preparation had the personal attention of the Chief Scout Executive. His greatest consideration in planning was the welfare of the individual boy. Much of the satisfaction that came to the boys from the thorough planning of the Jamboree should be credited to the efforts of the Chief Scout Executive."[80]

West rode in an open car with Roosevelt, and he was on the cover of *Time* magazine. "That the Boy Scouts of today are different . . . from the puny organization they were in 1910 is largely James West's doing."[81] The participants' manual, *Jamboreeing in Washington*, even suggested a pilgrimage to locations from West's youth: Columbia Hospital at 25th and L Sts, Washington City Orphan Home at 14th and S Sts., and Children's Hospital at 13th and W Sts. "All three institutions are still standing although the Washington City Orphan Home has been remodeled and is partially used for other purposes."[82] Bob West, now an Eagle Scout, led the Pledge of Allegiance at the Opening Ceremony that Dan Beard had opened by starting the council fire with flint and steel. The fire had been laid with wood from all 48 states. A Jamboree in the Nation's Capital was a publicity bonanza for the BSA and was fully exploited as such by the new Public Relations Service that portrayed boys as having fun and demonstrated to adults that the organization was indeed building character.

Meals were prepared in Section kitchens and brought to Troops in heater stacks. Consequently, there was no problem about segregated dining facilities. "Negro groups came from all the regions and were housed at the Jamboree in accord with the prevailing custom in the region from which they came. Negro boys from the southern cities were in separate troops, but in the midst of Scouts from their own territory. There was enthusiastic approval of the method of handling the troops."[83] There were no pictures of black American Scouts in the souvenir book. In the one group photo of the national staff, the two black men stood together at one edge.

The 1937 Jamboree was insured, as had been the one in 1935. West proudly reported that the insurance company had settled for just thirteen thousand dollars for damaged or lost items. The Scouts had borrowed 352,000 items from the Army and taken very good care of them.

After the National Jamboree, West accompanied the BSA contingent to the World Jamboree in the Netherlands, where he served as Camp Chief for the American contingent. Each American Scout received a copy of the Rose portrait of West, and West generously autographed them if asked. American Scouts demonstrated "Scoutcraft" rather than folklore (Indian dancing) and West took pride in having the highest standards of comfort, health, and safety in camp. "In Holland, it was a matter of great pride that our American delegation was judged to have the cleanest camp in the great cantonment and that in a country noted for well kept cities and spotless homes."[84] He complained to Beard that he had been snubbed by other national leaders until Baden-Powell personally intervened but he had positive words for Baden-Powell himself: "The Chief Scout confidentially told Mrs. West, as they sat reviewing the American demonstration in the arena, that it was the only real Scouting demonstration that he had seen in the arena up to that time. He graciously stayed through the whole show notwithstanding the fact that it went beyond his normal tea hour."[85]

West also attended the 10th World Conference and 3rd World Rover Moot in Scotland in 1939. There the sixth World Jamboree was scheduled for France in 1941. In July 1940 it was postponed until there was peace again in Europe.

Tyrant and Friend

Because of his position and his personality style, West always traveled with an aide. This was usually his personal stenographer, Tommy Murphy; however, if Murphy were unable to make a trip, another stenographer would be recruited. According to one of these men, West appeared to have well-organized responses to questions and enunciated clearly for the benefit of the stenographer. Some saw him as a tyrant. Willis Elliott was sent out to search for corona corona cigars at a brief train stop in a strange town. Roe Bartle observed West's knocking out a train window with his cane when the porter refused to open it for him.[86] Shaver recalled two episodes in his memoir. On one occasion Shaver had been able to turn in the return tickets and negotiate a lower train fare for a group of Scout Executives returning from a conference. With the extra money, he arranged for a private car, a porter, sandwiches, coffee, and a special box of chocolates for West. After West boarded the train, he seemed puzzled by the arrangements. Instead of praising Shaver, he "roared: 'Didn't you know you were handling National Council money? You are supposed to save every cent you can. Who authorized you to get the car and the sandwiches? I question whether you should be a deputy [regional executive]. You must do a better job in handling money.'" On another occasion, Shaver was to arrange the schedule for West's arrival at a meeting in Wisconsin. West had apparently forgotten it and had almost missed a Scout honor guard that had turned out to greet him. Although he had decided to tour the city without telling anyone, he insisted that "the man who handled those arrangements should have been fired."[87] At a meeting in Utah, an executive had forgotten to pack a green tie, so he wore a brown one with his uniform. Afterwards, West told the man's superior, "Hammond, I suggest you advise your assistant to get a green tie." The miscreant overheard and apologized. "I knew you'd notice, Chief, and I knew you'd say something about it." West shook his hand and replied, "I'm glad I didn't disappoint you."[88]

On the other hand, West was loyal to his close associates. When Ralph Nodine, Executive of Region 1, was taken seriously ill at the World Jamboree in 1937, West sent encouraging letters and telegrams to him and was supportive of his widow after Nodine's death. When Lorne Barkley was hospitalized in Utah, West actually visited him there.

Family members had a very different perspective, as the Chief was more relaxed at home. Goodman wrote about a episode when he and West were in the study in West's New Rochelle home one evening when daughter Marion came home late from a date: "When she came into the study to say goodnight, he rebuked her severely. Marion came over to his big chair, threw her arms affectionately around his neck, and said: 'Now Daddy, you wouldn't be cross with your little Marion, would you?' and she stooped down and kissed him. The man of decision and stern judgment wilted with a sheepish smile, and Marion trotted happily off to bed."[89]

West invited the staff and their families to an annual Christmas party at national headquarters. Observers never felt that West was comfortable at these and his major contribution to the party was to make a moving appeal for contributions to the *New York Times* "Neediest Child" program. He tried to be a good host, but it was obviously difficult for him.

Relationships

During 1938 West addressed Beard variously as "Dear Commissioner Beard" and "Dear Uncle Dan," sometimes as a friend and sometimes as a recalcitrant child. "I do believe at times you have made my job a wee bit more difficult without intending to do so, and I feel at times you have indicated a lack of appreciation of how earnestly all of us here have tried to add to your comfort and happiness and deal with you in a more than fair way."[90]

After a second stay at the Mayo Clinic, West wrote, "Thanks for your fine letter of the 27th. I am glad to tell you my health has improved and while I will be under the care of the tuberculosis experts for some months, I am rather confident I can lick my present troubles, as I have others.

I am happy to say that our family is quite well, except Helen had a recurrence of her previous trouble and has had to leave Vassar, much to our disappointment."[91]

West also reported about the other children. The ever-practical Marion attended Katherine Gibbs after graduating from Mount Holyoke and Bob was happy at Princeton. Arthur meanwhile had graduated from Yale Law School. The education and connections were good for the Wests because three of the children married into wealthy families. A family story has it that when Marion began dating a Catholic without money, West hired a private detective to find out about him. As it turned out, the boyfriend, Bill Higgins, was an agent for the Federal Bureau of Investigation. J. Edgar Hoover did not take kindly to such investigations and investigated West.[92] If there were such an investigation, nothing turned up because when the Fingerprinting merit badge was introduced in 1938, Hoover responded positively to West's request for a contribution to the pamphlet. Hoover also wrote an article entitled "Every Scout a future G-Man" for *Liberty* magazine in 1940.

In another letter to Beard in September, West lamented, "It is rather annoying to have to spend so much time on my back and give so much time to light treatments, but I am able to use about three out of every twelve hours on my back in reading material that has to be reviewed by me. So it has its compensations." [93] (Ultraviolet light therapy for non-pulmonary tuberculosis was common in the 1930s because it was thought to have bactericidal power and there was as yet no effective chemotherapy.)[94] "Wouldn't it be wonderful if you and I were thirty years younger and could start out with all the privileges and opportunities that present day conditions afford! We could do things that would make for a better America and a better world. Well, each of us has done his best and is doing his best and we will leave behind a record that will at least serve as a basis for more and better work for youth."[95]

Try Again

When Scout Executives gathered in Bretton Woods, New Hampshire in September, 1939 for the Seventh National Training Conference, West's friend, Roe Bartle, made the opening presentation to West:

> Three years ago Harold Williams became courageous and called him 'Uncle Jimmy.' I liked that. I have always thought of him since then as 'Uncle Jimmy' although I have never called him that (laughter). And when the plane was landing this afternoon, Colonel [Theodore] Roosevelt [Jr., Teddy's son] looked out the window and said, 'There's Jim West.' I liked that too.
>
> One of the fine things in coming to New York has been to know that there is a Jim West, and that there is an 'Uncle Jimmy,' if you please, coupled with that driving force and personality. And so the Committee felt they should have some way of expressing to him, making to him a gift. They wanted a gift that would be symbolic, one that would remind him of his men, of his flock. They wanted to make the gift of friendship; they wanted to make the gift of loyalty; they wanted to make the gift of responsiveness to all requests for service; they wanted to say to him, 'We honor you for what you are; and grateful for the privilege of being associated with you.'[96]

They gave him a scroll and a set of traveling bags. Colonel Roosevelt later added:

> We have been old friends and close friends, as he said, for years. Our friendship has been based on the only really firm foundation possible, that of great respect for the other's ideals and aims.
>
> The only friendship that really lasts and is worth while, is when two people are working for the same things, the things that they believe in and the things that they think are clean and decent and right and proper. That is what Jim West has been doing all his life.[97]

West must have been additionally gratified to receive a letter from Sir Percy Everett, Deputy Chief Commissioner for the United Kingdom, after the conference. Everett had been with Baden-Powell since Brownsea. He noted that he had initially been prejudiced against the "immensity and complexity of your organization and the fact that you depend so largely on a staff of paid executives;" however, he went on to say that that was the American way and that he liked the executives he had met. "Having met your Scout Executives personally and in Conference, any prejudice that I may have had about your system has been completely removed."[98]

Evolution

As the end of the decade drew near, the organizational phase of the Boy Scout Movement was nearly complete. By the end of 1938, 84.9% of potential districts had been organized in 536 functioning councils served by 1280 Scout Executives. The Executive Retirement Plan finally went into effect in February 1938 and a Group Life Insurance Plan began as well. Committees for training, advancement, camping and activities, health and safety, finance, and organization and extension were formed at national, regional, council, district, and troop committee levels. West did add a Research Division at the National level because "we have shown interest and regard for facts rather than opinion."[99] He remained very committed to statistics.

The Chief then turned to business consolidation. "We must never lose sight of the fact that, although we are a great social agency, it is necessary as a business organization that our financial record be thoroughly sound and indicate economical procedure."[100]

"Scouting must be conducted on a business-like basis."[101]

The Boy Scouts of America was already designing, manufacturing, and distributing badges and insignia as well as publishing over four hundred different books, pamphlets, and other pieces of literature. The organization then moved to totally control distribution of uniforms and equipment by licensing 1533 dealers and agents. Dealers carried stock while agents could only order material.[102]

The Chief Scout Executive was particularly proud of his National Executive Board:

> Not only do many of the men have records of continuous
> service but our attendance record is unusually high in
> the field of social, philanthropic, and educational work .
> . . Practically every member of the Executive Board [the
> exception was Beard] has always insisted upon paying his
> own expenses, not only in railroad fare, travel, and hotel
> bills in connection with attending board meetings, but
> even meals that are served incident to official business
> of the Boy Scouts of America. Furthermore, I believe
> that without exception, the members of our board take
> advantage of every opportunity to keep themselves
> informed, not only about our general operations,
> but about the details related to their own particular
> responsibility.[103]

Lee F. Hammer of the Russell Sage Foundation and a Board
member told West, "The way you have held your Executive Board and
National Council - the outstanding men of America - to give time and
devotion and money and their best ability to this cause is one of the
greatest tributes that I can hand to you today. You have achieved things,
old boy, and we're mighty proud of you."[104]

Financial responsibility was encouraged at the unit level as well
through the Troop Budget Plan or weekly dues. "The troop budget
plan has values to the individual boy from the standpoint of Scouting.
It makes it possible for the boy, by weekly payment of a small sum, to
feel that he is carrying his share of the load of the troop."[105]

Part of the troop budget was to be the provision of *Boys' Life* to
each Scout. The magazine was in trouble again. Circulation had dropped
from 300,000 to 96,000 per month. West attributed this to the advent of
comic books, now selling at the rate of two or three million per month.
Councils were given subscription quotas, and "*Boys' Life* week" was introduced to promote subscriptions as Christmas gifts. West also added
comics to *Boys' Life* and the Public Relations Service developed its own
daily strip for syndication. "Roy Powers, Eagle Scout" was launched
on May 10, 1937 and eventually appeared in 75 newspapers where, according to West, it "brings a true and wholesome picture of Scouting
to boyhood [and] will do much, it is believed, to raise standards of the
feature sections in newspapers where it appears."[106]

The Thirties

West felt the same about the movies, noting:

> I helped to organize the Motion Picture Public Relations
> Committee and was a member of the committee which
> pursued Colonel Jason S. Joy to serve as our Executive
> Officer in a definitely planned program to develop
> and maintain an open door so that the producers of
> motion pictures would have the benefit of criticism
> and cooperation of the thousands of people who, like
> myself, believed in motion pictures and had vision and
> faith for the development of a very influential and
> wholesome factor in the education of youth, as well as
> wholesome entertainment. Since that time there has
> been a constant, steady march forward.[107]

The shining example was a twelve part serial *Scouts to the Rescue*
starring Jackie Cooper. It was written by Irving Crump, Managing Editor of *Boys' Life*, and advertised as "cram-packed with stirring exploits
of a Boy Scout Horse Patrol." Mathiews reviewed it very positively.
The plot contained G-Men, Indians, buried treasure, and counterfeiters
- a typical Scout weekend camp. West praised it. "The Boy Scouts of
America congratulate Universal Pictures Inc. for its splendid and vividly
interesting contribution to our Scout members."[108] Part of the appeal
must have been that all the actors wore official Scout uniforms and carried all official Scout equipment. They looked like real Scouts.

In the Thirtieth Annual Report, West wrote: "The agitators, the
Communists, and other radicals have fought and gained here in America.
They are capitalizing on every advantage. In my judgment, they do
not constitute any great menace that should give us great concern . . .
the activity of the Communists has helped the Boy Scouts rather than
hinder it . . . We in Scouting are more determined than we were before
to do our job, to make our influence count because of these subversive
influences."[109] West asked the rhetorical question as to what America
could do and then provided *America's Answer*. In this large, spiral-bound
photo essay, West noted that:

> The dictators of Europe have not stopped with
> regimenting the youth of their own countries . . .

today they are spreading the propaganda of hate and intolerance to the four corners of the earth. Everywhere people are asking, 'What are we going to do about it? What can we do about it? How are we going to keep the real spirit of America alive in the Nation's youth?' AMERICA'S ANSWER lies in the country's greatest youth movement . . . over 1,000,000 boys who are dedicating themselves to the rights and responsibilities of American citizenship and to the principles of tolerance and human brotherhood . . . THAT MOVEMENT IS THE BOY SCOUTS OF AMERICA.[110]

In testimony before the House Unamerican Activities Committee, West quoted his response to a letter from "militant Christian patriots" protesting the presence of a Jewish entertainer at a California Court of Honor. West wrote, "[We] would be neglecting our fundamental obligation, if in all our public gatherings we did not welcome and encourage participation of the representatives of all religious groups. It is our conception that the principle of religious liberty is inseparably interwoven with the fundamental principles of American democracy." He added, "Some of our best Scouts are Jewish boys."[111] West considered himself a patriot.

West also still considered himself an educator. To Henry W. Holmes at the Harvard School of Education, West wrote:

When it comes to such things as preaching, marching, competing for prizes, etc., well, frankly we just don't make much of any of these methods. As I have said, we believe in practice rather than preachment. When it comes to parades, we would much rather have Scouts manning First Aid Stations on the side line or helping to keep the crowd back. When it comes to competition, we have found increasing success in setting up a plan so that Troops and Patrols enter into competition not so much against other Troops and Patrols as against standards of excellence in which each group that makes good can come out a winner.[112]

On October 25, 1939 West actually sent a congratulatory telegram to the Girl Scouts on their Twenty-fifth Anniversary. "The American people recognize the importance of every agency that helps develop the girlhood of the nation."[113] Boy Scouts even helped out at the Girl Scout Chalet at the New York Worlds Fair. But, in his heart of hearts, West was still waiting for the Girl Scouts to merge with the Camp Fire Girls. "From the standpoint of what is best for America, and what is best for the girls of America, there can be little discussion of what ought to be done. The main problem in the past has been the attitude of mind of some of the members of the governing board of the Girl Scouts. So far as the rank and file of both organizations is concerned they have over the years been very receptive to the idea of amalgamation."[114]

Some of West's ideas would never change. Nevertheless, even with war in Europe, the thirties ended on a positive note with a total membership of 1,391,831 on December 31, 1939 as Cubs and their Den Mothers were finally counted as members.

Notes

[1] Twenty-first Annual Report of the BSA page 13
[2] 12/03/31 letter in BSA Archives
[3] Forward to "The Troop Program and Scouting Tenure" 1934
[4] Proceedings of 6th National Training Conference (NTC) 1936 page 523
[5] Beard LOC 134 5/15/31
[6] Beard LOC 134 6/25/31
[7] 3/09/31 letter in BSA Archives
[8] Beard LOC 134 Copy of relevant part of 11/26/30 will
[9] Beard LOC 134 9/09/31
[10] Beard LOC 134 9/26/31
[11] Beard LOC 134 10/07/31
[12] *Scouting* 7/32 page 197
[13] Beard LOC 135 4/20/32
[14] See Money, John. *The Destroying Angel*. Buffalo: Prometheus 1985
[15] Beard LOC 135 5/05/33
[16] Beard LOC 135 1/11/34
[17] Proceedings 6th NTC 1936 page 59
[18] Twenty-second Annual Report of the BSA page 33
[19] Ibid page 6
[20] *Boys' Life* 8/32 page 22
[21] *Boys' Life* 11/31 page 3
[22] *Boys' Life* 11/30 page 69
[23] Twenty-fifth Annual Report of the BSA page 13
[24] Twenty-fourth Annual Report of the BSA page 66
[25] "The Troop Program and Scout Tenure" 1934
[26] *Handbook, Boy Rangers of America*. New York 1925. page 14
[27] Ibid page 87
[28] Proceedings of 3rd NTC 1924 page 201
[29] Beard LOC 132 5/26/26
[30] Beard LOC 109 4/20/25
[31] Proceedings 4th NTC 1926 page 299
[32] *Handbook, Boy Rangers of America*. Page 28
[33] Proceedings 3rd NTC 1924 page 205
[34] Proceedings 6th NTC 1936 page 731
[35] *Scout Executive* 11/30 page 4
[36] Beard LOC 109 1/15/30
[37] Beard LOC 135 3/10/34
[38] Twenty-sixth Annual Report of the BSA page 16
[39] Block, Nelson. *A Thing of the Spirit: The Life of E. Urner Goodman*. Irving, TX: BSA, 2000. page 49

The Thirties

40 *Boys' Life* 3/32 page 22
41 *Boys' Life* 9/34 page 20
42 *Boys' Life* 1/35 page 22
43 *Boys' Life* 5/31 page 22
44 *Boys' Life* 8/34 page 50
45 Testimony to Senate Commerce Committee May 1934 quoted in the Twenty-Fourth
    Annual Report of the BSA. Page 62 ff
46 Twenty-sixth Annual Report of the BSA page 14
47 Twenty-eighth Annual Report of the BSA page 14
48 Beard LOC 98 9/25/34
49 *Boys' Life* 7/27 page 39
50 Undated press release in Lindbergh Archives at Missouri Historical Society (MHS)
51 *Boys' Life* 8/27 page 25
52 5/06/29 telegram to West, MHS
53 7/28 telegram to West, MHS
54 copy at Missouri Historical Society
55 *Boys' Life* 5/31 page 66
56 Quoted by Berg, A. Scott. *Lindbergh.* New York: Berkley, 1999. page 247
57 While he was away, Baden-Powell rented his home in England. The ad in the July 1934
    Headquarters Gazette offered Pax Hill with 5 reception rooms, 11 bedrooms,
    3 baths, 11 acres, 6 maids, 2 gardeners, and 1 chauffeur but no price was
    given.
58 *Boys' Life* 9/35 page 21
59 Beard LOC 136 1/03/36
60 *Scouting* 2/60 page 39
61 See Hillcourt, William. *Norman Rockwell's World of Scouting.* New York: Henry N.
    Abrams, 1977
62 Beard LOC 136 1/08/36
63 Beard LOC 136 8/21/36
64 See Trine R. W. *The Best of Ralph Waldo Trine.* New York: Bobbs-Merrill, 1957 page
    11
65 Fisher's 1935 tribute in BSA Archives
66 Twenty-Eighth Annual Report of the BSA page 13
67 *Scouting for Rural Boys.* BSA 1938. page 248
68 *Boys' Life* 2/35 page 36
69 *Boys' Life* 12/38 page 1
70 *Boys' Life* 2/35 page 21
71 Proceedings of 6th NTC 1936 page 7
72 Ibid page 8
73 Ibid page 381
74 Beard LOC 136 4/20/36
75 Beard LOC 136 5/06/36
76 *Boys' Life* 9/35 page 50
77 Beard LOC 136 10/15/37
78 Beard LOC 136 10/16/37
79 Beard LOC 136 12/19/36
80 Lorne Barclay in 28th Annual Report of the BSA page 55
81 *Time* 7/12/37 page 15

[82] Ibid page 17
[83] Twenty-eighth Annual Report of the BSA page 194
[84] *Boys' Life* 10/37 page 50
[85] Beard LOC 136 9/14/37
[86] Don Green, personal communication
[87] Shaver, W. W. *A Pioneer's Journal of Scouting Stories*. Printed privately 1977
[88] Monroe, K. "Jim West: Scouting's gruff genius" *Scouting* 11-12/74 page 41
[89] Goodman, E.U. "James E. West as I knew him" *Now and Then* 4/4 page 1
[90] Beard LOC 137 1/22/38
[91] Beard LOC 137 5/31/38
[92] This could not be confirmed because of an inadequate response from the FBI to a request under the Freedom of Information Act.
[93] Beard LOC 137 9/20/38
[94] See Webb, G. *Tuberculosis*. New York: Hoeber, 1936
[95] Beard LOC 137 11/01/38
[96] Proceedings of the 7th NTC 1939 page 16
[97] Ibid page 22
[98] Beard LOC 137 11/17/39
[99] Twenty-eighth Annual Report of the BSA page 14
[100] Twenty-ninth Annual Report of the BSA page 9
[101] *Scout Administrator* 2/35 page 8
[102] Twenty-eighth Annual Report of the BSA page 26
[103] Twenty-ninth Annual Report of the BSA page 6
[104] *Scout Administrator* 1/36 page 1
[105] Twenty-eighth Annual Report page 22
[106] Ibid page 131
[107] *Boys' Life* 12/38 page 26
[108] *Boys' Life* 1/39 page 16
[109] Thirtieth Annual Report of the BSA page 45
[110] *America's Answer*. BSA undated and unpaginated
[111] Twenty-ninth Annual Report of the BSA page 68
[112] Beard LOC 137 9/27/39
[113] Beard LOC 137 10/25/39
[114] Beard LOC 137 11/04/39

Chapter 7

End of the Reign

George Fisher predicted that retirement would be the most difficult transition that West ever made. He was right. West's activities became even more frenetic as that time approached. He busied himself with the World's Fair, editorials, editing, War Service projects, "Less Chance Scouting," and testimonials. This made his inevitable retirement even more wrenching.

The Fair

Scout participation at the New York World's Fair in 1939 and 1940 was the last large public display during West's tenure as Chief Scout Executive. The management had invited the Boy Scouts of America to maintain a demonstration and service corps at the Fair. West accepted but asked the Fair management to pay half the costs of development and one third of the cost of food for those on duty. Management agreed. As they had at the National Jamboree in 1937, Scout troops came from around the country and camped on site. Only the Scouts, Army, Navy, and Marines were allowed to do this. 3948 Scouts and Scouters served at the Fair in 1939 and 3151 in the shorter season of 1940. The Scouts served as event and department aides, honor guards, color guards, ushers, and guides in addition to maintaining a model camp and exhibits.

Dan Beard turned ninety in 1940 and West organized a birthday party for him on June 22 as part of the Boy Scout Day activities at the World's Fair. West had previously orchestrated a rally for 63,000 Scouts at the 1939 Fair, the largest Scout gathering ever held to date. Despite intense promotion, the 1940 attendance did not exceed the 1939 total, and, rather than admit that, the national office consistently reported the number as "thousands." Characteristically, West did not want to publicize any figures that might be interpreted as a drop in interest in the Scouting program.

Dueling Founders, Again

West considered Beard a friend but the reciprocal feeling is not as clear. Beard had reestablished a relationship with Seton and made this remarkably revisionist statement in 1939: "This party started a whispering campaign, which told Seton that Dan Beard had said thus and so, and incited his ire; and then told Dan Beard that Seton had said this and that, angering him. In the end he put you out of Scouting, but thank the Good Lord, I was not there and took no part in that."[1] Could Seton have believed that?

Seton kept in touch with Scouting. Scouting kept in touch with him but did not acknowledge his earlier connection to it. In March 1927, *Boys' Life* noted that Seton "the famous Woodcrafter" was Honorary President of the Greenwich [Connecticut] Council. In December 1930 an ad for Seton's *Library of Pioneering and Woodcraft* made no mention of his earlier contributions. When a Seton story, "The Mackenzie River Ghost" appeared in *Boys' Life* in December 1938, there was no affiliation after his name. Seton was aware of West's illness in 1938 when he commented to Robinson that his problem with West might soon solve itself. "I do not know who will take West's place, but it will be one of three men, I am told, every one of them favorable to my views; that is, they want more of my thought and activities in their program."[2]

Beard continued to put forth his version of history. In an undated letter to West, he wrote: "Look over my *Buckskin Book*, at letters, dates, etc., and my book *Boy Pioneers*, all of which, with the exception of a few stunts was written and printed before Baden-Powell 'cribbed' the idea."[3] In 1940 Beard promoted this perspective in his rambling, disorganized autobiography, *Hardly a Man is now Alive*. West was successful in having it changed. He wrote to Baden-Powell in a letter addressed "Dear Chief:" "As a matter of fact in the last two years we have had almost as much trouble with Uncle Dan as we have had with Seton, based on material submitted in his biography. Thanks to our relationship to Colonel Roosevelt, Vice President of the publishing firm of Doubleday, Doran which handled Uncle Dan's book the material related to Scouting was considerably modified, although it is still inaccurate in spots."[4]

West had even more success in purging Seton's autobiography, *Trail of an Artist Naturalist.* As he cabled Baden-Powell, "Happy to report that publishers [Scribners] have agreed eliminate all reference to Scouting from Seton's biography. Cordial greetings."[5] Seton sent copies of the offending chapter on Scouting to Beard and Robinson, so it has not been lost to history. Seton claimed to be writing the spiritual history of Scouting as opposed to Murray's organizational one. "West had commissioned his assistant, E. S. Martin to write the history of the Boy Scouts. Martin assembled his material some of which he got from my copies of Baden-Powell's letters and then came out flat footed and said there is no question that the fundamental ideas of the Boy Scouts and all its valuable activities were supplied by Seton long before Baden-Powell appeared in the field. West was furious; he took the whole thing out of Martin's hands, and then gave it all to W. D. Murray, who has always been hostile to me."[6] Seton wrote in the draft that he had visited Baden-Powell in 1906 and given him a copy of the *Birch Bark Roll* and that, over the next two years Baden-Powell had sent him forty-two letters as he developed his program. Seton had saved the letters:

> I make this emphatic statement: In my opinion there is not an important idea in *Scouting For Boys* that I did not publish years ago in *Two Little Savages, The Birch Bark Roll,* and my Woodcraft and Scouting articles of which I furnished him with copies. The only important changes he made were to add a little military drill, give things new names and assume their authorship for himself. In his own words [letter of 31st October 1906] the schemes are 'practically identical.' "He [Baden-Powell] has eliminated all things of the aesthetic and spiritual world . . . my aim was to make a man—his was to make a soldier.[7]

West took one final opportunity to honor William D. Boyce as the founder of Scouting in America at the dedication of the Boyce memorial in Ottawa, Illinois on June 21, 1941. The memorial design, a McKenzie statue next to the grave, had been approved by West and paid for by one dollar contributions from over 9000 Scouts and Scouters. West's speech was not recorded, so, if he said anything with regard to the ultimate thickness of the nonexistent 1909 fog, it remains unknown.

Dan Beard died on June 11, 1941 and West led the Theodore Roosevelt Pilgrimage in Oyster Bay for the first and only time on October 18, 1941. In his speech he paid tribute to "Uncle Dan" and his ideals of good citizenship. Without its founder and with war restrictions, the Roosevelt Pilgrimage faded away over the next few years. Seton died in 1946 without further contact with West.

Books and Other Business

In addition to "editing" outside autobiographies, West signed off on every important document that came from within the organization as well. "This department [Editorial Service] is responsible for editing and approving every piece of copy produced by the national staff newspaper stories and radio scripts no less than periodicals and pamphlets. Further, it has the power to ascertain the value of every published item bearing the imprint of scout headquarters and to decide when a printed piece has outlived its usefulness and should be revised or discarded. Often, however, responsibilities of editing, as well as of writing and production, were farmed out to other divisions and services. As a final step, the Chief Scout Executive, or in his absence, a delegated authority, must add his approval to production items - particularly to more important ones. This again applies to the output of the Public Relations Service as well as to other services and divisions."[8] West had not loosened his control.

In 1941 the Research and Statistical Service was created with George Ehler as director. When Ehler retired later that year, F. N. Cole became Research Director and Assistant to the Chief Scout Executive. Cole began testing programs and techniques in one or two "demonstration councils" in each region. He also tried to boost membership statistics as a "patriotic service in this national emergency." One result of the tests was West's decision to focus on "orderly exit" and to drop the designation of "separated" for Scouts who had left the program. If they had not died, dropped, transferred to another unit, or advanced to Senior Scouting, they were encouraged to become "Junior Alumni" who pledged to remain "Once a Scout, always a Scout."[9] This kept up the membership numbers.

Also in 1941, the Field Service reported that 96.6% of potential districts were now organized as "we have progressively organized to bring supervised Scouting closer to the boy."[10] The business division provided a new service and additional income by selling handicraft supplies to summer camps. With regard to camps, the Boy Scouts of America also made an exception to a long-standing policy to discourage federal subsidies by accepting several former Civilian Conservation Corps camps that were being given to non-profit organizations.

The national office was also distributing press kits to over 8500 local newspapers. These articles were sent out on a regular schedule, so they were not timely and they had no local slant or color. Small wonder that they were not widely used. As part of the public relations effort, West was also negotiating with Warner Brothers to develop a feature film about the benefits of Scouting. Like so many of the potential Scout movies before it, this one was never produced.

Reading guidance was still an important part of the mission. Over two million copies of the seventy-three titles in the *Every Boy's Library* series had been sold by 1940, but by then, only nineteen remained in print. They were expensive books; this was the Depression; there was not much discretionary spending on books. During *Boys' Life* Week in December 1940, the BSA began promoting the "Boy Scout Bookshelf." The national office recommended that every boy should buy and read the *Bible*, the *Scout Handbook*, and ten other classics (Sandburg's *Abraham Lincoln Grows Up*, Hagedorn's *Boy's Life of Theodore Roosevelt*, *Captains Courageous*, *Huckleberry Finn*, *Tom Sawyer*, *Ivanhoe*, *Last of the Mohicans*, *The Microbe Hunters*, *Robinson Crusoe*, and *Treasure Island*.) Other titles were to be added. None were. The passion for guided reading cooled after West retired.

Boys' Life had a new format, with "The Editor Speaks" moved up to page 3. "Establishing the inspirational quality of the magazine throughout and setting the tone of each issue, the editorial page by Dr. James E. West has become the opening feature of the publication."[11] "Scout World," the section on Good Turns and awards, no longer contained text other than captions on the pictures. West was in at least one picture in nearly every issue. The Editor even changed his mind about comics:

> I was interested in the reaction to a page of comics that
> we have added to *Boys' Life*. 126 out of 240 replying felt
> that these comics added to the value of *Boys' Life*.
>
> Over the years, I have frequently characterized many
> of the comics as one of the most harmful influences
> in the life of America. While there has been great
> improvement, still too often they glorify deceit,
> disloyalty, and many things harmful to growing children.
> I am conscious, however, that there are few young
> people in America who are not interested in comics,
> regardless of what lessons they teach. The test from a
> child's point of view is solely from the standpoint of its
> entertainment value.[12]

Pragmatism prevailed, and West really had seen the boys' point
of view.

Making the Most of Yourself, a collection of West's editorials, was
published by Appleton-Century in 1941. With titles like "It can be
done!" "Stick to it!" and "Aim high!" it was unfailingly positive and
reflected West's own view of the reasons for his success. The ad for the
book led with "Are These Your Questions: Do you lack determination?
Find it hard to make decisions? Lose confidence in yourself? Forget
how to smile? Then read *Making the Most of Yourself*."[13] The publisher
ran a contest in *Boys' Life* for the best reviews of the book by those aged
12 to 14, 15 to 17, and 18 to 80. West published the winning reviews.

In addition to dispensing advice in his editorials, West kept up a
massive correspondence, relating as best he could to Scouts and former
Scouts:

> It has been my happy privilege to maintain a personal
> correspondence with nearly four thousand young men.
> I began this correspondence and maintained it because
> I first of all had a very deep personal interest in these
> boys as I have in all Scouts. I wanted to know too their
> ambitions, the goals toward which they were striving in
> college and after college and just how much their Scout
> training and early association were helping them toward

achieving their ambitions. And I wanted to bring to their attention the Senior Scout Citizenship Declaration so that they might more consciously become members of the great Scout alumni.

I knew that I would get back some fine letters. I knew that many of these boys would attest to the fact that Scouting has done much for them both in building character and in training them as fine upstanding American citizens but I was truly pleased, if not indeed happily amazed at the wholehearted enthusiasm and agreement of all these boys that Scouting had been the most moving influence in their lives toward character building, outside of their own homes.[14]

In addition, West had always sent a letter of congratulations to each new Eagle Scout. These form letters included good wishes, statistics, and the hope that the Scout would go on to help others along the way. In 1941 he added a plug for the "Program of Action for Strengthening and Invigorating Democracy" and in 1942 began to close with, "If at any time I can be helpful to you in a personal problem, I hope that you will write to me."[15] West might have been thinking about something to do in retirement and he sincerely wanted to maintain contact with former Scouts.

Revising History, Again

Colonel Roosevelt wrote a glowing introduction to *Making the Most of Yourself*. Board President Head contributed another stirring tribute in the January 1941 issue of *Boys' Life*. The Rose portrait of West was the January illustration on the official Boy Scout calendar and it was also added to the official Wood Burning Kit. The lead story in the *Doc Savage* comic for May was "Only in America could this have happened, the legend of James E. West." Tributes were gathered together in *Thirty Years of Service*, which was printed privately "through the courtesy of friends." The tributes included several stories that had appeared only in the previous five years and featured West as an outdoorsman:

> I know from my own experience that it is possible to have a joyful experience in the out of doors in spite of handicaps. One of the unique experiences of my boyhood was my Saturday afternoon pilgrimages through the woods of what is now a park—then wild country. I lived in an institution for orphan children. I was the oldest boy, and I developed a scheme whereby those who had certain records for cooperation in doing their chores, had the privilege of going off on a Saturday afternoon for a hike: and it was some hike! We did not have money for carfare. We did not have money for grub. But we had real adventure. It was not an unusual thing for me to take thirty or forty boys on these trips.[16]

"Cooking has interested me all my life. I learned how to cook in the open as a boy, when I used to take a crowd of younger children into the woods on Saturday afternoon hikes. Since then I have cooked over campfires and kitchen stoves, with equipment ranging from the latest gadgets to a tin pail and a jack-knife and I still think cooking is fun."[17] He would later say proudly that he prepared the turkey stuffing for the family Thanksgiving dinner. He did not say that his cook prepared the rest of the meal.

"Some of the most worth while days of my boyhood I spent with a group of younger children whom I had organized to go on scheduled hikes the year round. We had to keep moving in order to keep warm in winter. There were many periods when there was no opportunity for any kind of snow or ice sports, but we used vigorous games —Hare and Hounds, Tug of War, Relay Races, and found real adventure. We came back tingling with life, all set to go again."[18]

The tributes did not repeat the improbable claim that "as a boy I saved to buy a rifle and shot it in the woods." Specific incidents such as his learning to ride a bicycle and defending the boy charged with stealing his car rose to almost mythic proportions. The only heroic event that occurred after West became Chief Scout Executive involved cooking:

> We [West and Lorillard Spencer, Commissioner for
> Manhattan] arrived in camp [Hunter's Island] just as
> the buses were unloading. We were met by the Camp
> Director and told that the cook and his assistants
> had walked out. And there were 150 hungry boys!
> Fortunately the cooks had left their caps and aprons.
> A survey of the personnel available revealed that there
> was not a single person equal to the occasion of cooking
> for such a large crowd. I volunteered, donned the cook's
> cap and apron, and organizing a small group of older
> boys, we had our dinner at the scheduled hour lamb
> chops, French fried potatoes, stewed tomatoes, cocoa,
> ice cream and cake.[19]

West was never an outdoorsman. Contrary to Seton's 1915 assessment, West had seen the blue sky; however, contrary to his own
view, the boys from the orphanage were not his first Scout troop. To
paraphrase Beard, West was a businessman and a good one. If West were
preparing to replace Beard as the buckskin sage, then he was going to
be disappointed.

Tributes and Testimonials

West was very proud when the Boy Scouts of America celebrated
its thirtieth anniversary. "I am of the opinion that never in the history
of America has any agency - and I say this without reservation - enjoyed
such good repute, such high regard as does the Boy Scouts of America
today. That is based on a record of thirty years of progress, thirty years
of vitality on the part of millions participating and millions giving
leadership in a way that as been a living testimony to the values of the
game of Scouting."[20]

A childhood friend, Frank J. Hogan paid this tribute to West:

> What has Dr. West contributed to this marvelous
> success of an ideal? First, his sound legal training, which
> gave to Scouting an enduring foundation and an orderly
> government; second, his broad and understanding
> humanity which makes him his brother's keeper; third,
> his great executive ability, which has made him a genius

in picking the right man for every task; fourth, his capacity for action, prompt, dynamic, tireless; and fifth, a 'vision splendid.'

So tonight, while you still live, James West, we say to you that every time there are Boy Scouts within your vision's range; or whenever hereafter you review a Scout parade, or attend a gathering anywhere of any part of that organization, you need but look around you to see the enduring monument which will keep alive always in the hearts of America the memory of the life you have lived and are living.[21]

To this West replied, "Here in the City of Washington, there were so many agencies, so many institutions, and so many generous-hearted people, so many people who 'cared,' so many people who wanted to extend a helping hand, that any person, who had the opportunity that I had and didn't take advantage of it, must certainly have been an ingrate or a rather worthless human being."[22]

Another tribute came from Deputy Chief Scout Executive George Fisher. "The institution is a lengthened shadow of the individual." He described West with phrases such as "absorbed in work," "man of action," "self-confident," and "believer in organization."[23] West responded proudly, "In thirty years we have had only two organizational problems that have gone to the Executive Board; that is because the organization has really been MANAGED."[24]

On a different occasion, Fisher quoted West's response at the dedication of a flagpole in his honor at the Washington City Orphan Home (now called Hillcrest):

I am here today taking part in this ceremony somewhat as a symbol and interested frankly only to the extent that it will serve a useful purpose to those who may through [this] incident and what may be said about it, have their own attention brought to the fact that if a boy in America, anywhere in America, has the ambition and makes the effort, because America is what it is, it is within his power with the help of God, to go almost any place that he has the imagination and vision to seek.

> That to me is the glorious thing about an occasion of
> this character; that is a justification of our American
> way of life and our democracy.[25]

West was a very proud man, and such attempts at modesty never quite rang true.

In 1941 West received another honorary doctorate, this time an LLD from Hamilton College. "You have seen it [the Boy Scouts of America] bring into the lives of countless American boys a joyousness which you in your own boyhood knew but fleetingly; and you have seen it nurture a physical and spiritual defense for democracy which in these years of national peril may be one of its greatest strengths."[26]

West also received the Gold Medal for Distinguished Service to Humanity from the National Institute of Social Services. The citation read, "To Dr. James E. West, author, editor, and lecturer, in recognition of distinctive social services to humanity. [He] has devoted his life to helping build higher character in youth and train them for citizenship through many agencies and especially through the Boy Scouts of America which has been developed under his leadership and has enriched the lives of more than nine million persons."[27] Also honored were Wendell Wilkie (public utilities executive) and Carrie Chapman Catt (great champion of women's rights.)

1941 was West's thirtieth year on the job, but also the year he turned 65. In anticipation, the Executive Board had formed a "Special Committee on Operations and Personnel of the National Office," about which West commented, "I want to express appreciation to the Board for the action creating this Committee. I think it will be a very wise procedure. I want to say further that I shall, in the light of the circumstances, do everything in my power not only to cooperate with this Committee but with the Retirement Committee in making effective the wishes of the Board."[28]

On West's sixty-fifth birthday, President Roosevelt wrote to him:

> During these perilous times I am more conscious than
> ever of the patriotism of our Boy Scouts and the strength
> of their leadership. To you belongs much of the credit
> for the effectiveness of Scouting in this country. I desire

therefore to take this means, on your birthday, and on your thirtieth anniversary as Chief Scout Executive to tell you how much we appreciate your accomplishments in behalf of American boyhood.

Your service to Scouting over the years emphasized the effectiveness of the American way of providing equal opportunity to youth. You have, through your work, rendered your country great service.[29]

When Murray completed his official history of the BSA, he down-played West's autocratic role and made the organization appear more democratic than it really was. There was also to have been a separate biography of West. H. W. Hurt spent at least two official years gathering data for the book. Dutton, the publisher, originally identified Burr Leyson as the potential author but then switched to Herman Hagedorn. Hagedorn wrote this note to West on October 29, 1940, "I have a feeling that, when we had lunch together a week ago, I misrepresented what I really wanted to say and probably seemed merely insulting when what I actually wanted to do was to find out whether that in you which seemed to be vanity and the hunger to dominate was not actually compensation for a certain timorousness surviving from a difficult boyhood. I have myself suffered from a kind of inferiority which expresses itself in me in less attractive and effective forms. God knows I have no right and no reason to sit in judgment, or to throw the first stone."[30] Hagedorn agreed to write the book the next month.[31] His secretary, Miss Westhoff combed through hospital records and vital statistics to get details of West's youth, but Hagedorn's psychological premise, while probably correct, has yet to appear in published form.

"God Bless America"

In 1940 composer Irving Berlin wrote to the Chief Scout Executive, "What I want to know is if it is your fault or my fault that only within the last few months I have had an understanding of what the Scout movement is actually doing for America? Now, whose fault was it? I had the Broadway interpretation of Scouting, which was to take it not very seriously, a recreation program, giving the boys a good time. But, man alive, you are doing something more than that. You are building the very fiber of America. You are the lifeblood of America, you and your Scouts."[32] West generously responded that the fault had been his. Berlin then established the "God Bless America Fund" with the perpetual royalties from his popular song. Three trustees, Gene Tunney, Gen. Roosevelt, and Herbert B. Swope, would decide how to help the Boy Scouts, Girl Scouts, and Camp Fire Girls reach out to children in "low income areas." For the Boy Scouts, local councils submitted proposals to West, who approved them and sent them along to the trustees. Councils had to agree to match the grants and hire an executive for a year, and $65,000 was awarded in the first three years. "Less Chance Scouting" came to include not only inner-city black and white youths, but Indians in boarding schools, immigrant groups such as Poles in Buffalo, and rural communities such as those in Maine. The majority of target groups, however, do seem to have been black.[33]

War

As early as July 1940 the Boy Scouts of America was one of sixteen national organizations calling for its membership and all United States citizens to sign a pledge to strengthen and invigorate democracy. This was under the auspices of the Citizenship Educational Service, and the organizations included the BSA, Boys' Clubs, YMCA, YWCA, and Camp Fire Girls, but not the Girl Scouts. In contrast to Nazism, Communism, and Fascism, "the preservation of liberty rests upon the affirmation of the dignity of the individual and the acceptance of individual responsibility by every citizen of our land."[34] West wanted each council and troop to sign the pledge to "be prepared" but not to engage in military training.[35] Being in uniform was also important. "To be in spirit with the state of national emergency and the Scout program for 'Strengthening and Invigorating Democracy,' the Boy Scout Uniform plays a vital role. Today's national preparedness program calls for action, again. Scouts take what comes in their stride. Scouts stand out in many manly qualities. Their quick recognition, however, is always their Official Uniform."[36]

At the Advertising Club in New York City in a speech entitled "A million men in the making," West said: "We do not believe that military training as such is as valuable to boys of Scout age as is the program of Scouting, the program which utilizes the boy's natural interest in the great out-of-doors, in nature and all of the beauties of nature, and makes it possible for him to go on hikes into the woods, to explore, to go camping, and through experiences, develop self-reliance, resourcefulness, and ability to take care of himself and stand on his own feet, and, yes, able to give a helping hand to those in need."[37] This position was essentially the same one that he held during World War I, but after the United States entered World War II, West changed his mind and approved more militaristic activities.

Scouts had already participated in a number of Good Turns, so it was natural for West to telegraph President Roosevelt on December 8, 1941 to offer the services of one and one-half million Scouts:

> The efforts of the Boy Scouts of America during the last World War demonstrated that there are many projects which can be appropriately and successfully undertaken by boys of Scout age and with Scout training. Heretofore, we have happily responded to your personal request to distribute posters publicizing Defense Savings Bonds and Stamps, and to participate in the aluminum collection. Our efforts in the waste paper collection currently in operation, and in the Civilian Defense Program will be further intensified. It will be our earnest purpose to embrace to the full measure of our capacity any and all other opportunities to render further service to our country.[38]

To the Scout Executives, West said, "Our happiness and satisfaction at the Christmas season must come from our faith in God, in the ideals of our country, and in the righteousness of the cause to which we shall gladly devote all our strength and resources, under the leadership of the President of the United States."[39]

To the Scouts, West wrote that their first priority was to carry on the Scout program and to replace lost leaders and then "let us each highly resolve that in view of the need of America today we shall, as a contribution to the defense of our country, do everything within our power to extend the influence of this great Movement." [40]

Scouts were clearly identified as a group that could be called to community service in a time of need. Scouts collected ten and one-half million pounds of aluminum in 1941, thirty million pounds of scrap rubber in 1942, and, throughout the war, they collected fifty million pounds of waste paper. West signed an agreement with the Office of Civilian Defense so that Scouts in every community, under the supervision of the local Civil Defense Council, could assist emergency medical units and serve as fire watchers and messengers.

As "dispatch bearers," Scouts distributed a vast amount of government literature, including 1,607,500 posters promoting US Savings Bonds and Stamps for Defense and twenty-two million copies of "What You Should Know About Wartime Price Control," as well as "Divide and Conquer," a pamphlet designed to expose Axis propaganda strategy to diminish civilian morale. Scouts helped the Red Cross and participated in such projects as Razor Blades for Britain and the Victory Book Campaign (ten million good books for the Armed Forces). They built scale model planes for Navy training.

Scouts also planted gardens. "The immediate aims of our home gardening are to increase the vitamin intake of the general public, to free some of the rolling stock now transporting food from farm to consumer, to conserve through reduction in commercial canning, to supplement the family income and—vitally important—to free commercially grown fruits and vegetables for our armed forces and the needs of the United Nations everywhere."[41] West went on to note, "I myself, am considering extending my own garden, and recommend this practice to everyone who can. In fact, I am going further in the food production program and will raise chickens this year."[42] He had done that in his youth, but it is unlikely that he would want to revisit that orphanage experience again.

Franklin D. Roosevelt wrote, "Each and every Scout has reason to feel proud of the part he has as a member of Uncle Sam's team to help us win the war."[43] But service projects were not enough for some Scouts. They wanted to do more. To the "Boys in Wartime" survey conducted by the newly organized Statistical Service in New York and New Jersey early in 1942, sixty five percent reported that they wanted more active service.[44] West promoted the new Air Scout program (education, not flying) through articles in *Boys' Life* and specific aviation-oriented merit badge pamphlets and manuals throughout 1942, and he championed a National Defense Program for Scouts. This not only included collection, dispatch, production, and conservation as noted but also emergency service training and mobilization, as well as the decidedly more militant Boy Scout High School Victory Corps and Pre-Ranger Training.

The Emergency Service Corps consisted of older boys who had to be physically fit, qualified for appropriate merit badges, and trained for emergency response. Each Scout troop was to have a plan for both General and Immediate Mobilization, so that the unit could gather in case of emergency. The local council, district, or troop itself could call for a mobilization. Cubs could not participate.

In 1942 the Commissioner of the US Office of Education asked all High Schools to develop a Victory Corps, a voluntary program to include air service, land service, sea service, production service, and community service. West quickly offered the Scouting program as a way to meet all these needs: Air Scouting, Senior Scouting, Sea Scouting, industrial and agricultural merit badges, and vocational merit badges. Commissioner J. W. Studebaker and President Roosevelt enthusiastically accepted the offer.

Pre-Ranger Training was different. Its goals were "to teach Scouts by experience seventeen or more of the skills most important for them to know should they eventually enter one of the armed services things that can't possibly be learned sufficiently well by men after they are inducted; to give them a wide variety of training in self-reliance and personal discipline; to bring them home alive and victorious."[45] The skills included the usual axemanship, cooking, camping, first aid and signaling as well as map reading, stalking, rifle marksmanship, and "wartime aquatics." To the end of his tenure as Chief Scout Executive, West would insist that Scouting was not military and that all these programs simply provided skills to make boys better citizens and, only incidentally, better soldiers. Pre-Ranger Training seemed to go beyond that definition.

The professional service of the BSA was hard hit by the war. At the end of 1942 twenty-five percent (352 out of 1375) of the executives were in military service. Older men were recruited to replace them and more work fell on the remaining volunteers. As always, West saw this loss of staff as a recruiting opportunity. "Thanks to their efforts [volunteer leaders] in the midst of this great war, the Scout movement is in high gear. It was never better organized, never operating more effectively, never better understood by the American people. There never was a better opportunity to secure adequate financial resources to carry on. There never was a time when more boys wanted to be Scouts."[46]

On a more practical note, West wrote: "Immediately following the outbreak of the war, a committee was appointed to develop ways and means of protecting the personnel, property, and records of the Boy Scouts of America in the event of an air raid on the City of New York."[47] This included shelter zones, first aid stations, and metal filing cabinets.

Resistance

Despite his promise to cooperate with the Retirement Committee, West resisted the inevitable. First, he negotiated a one-year extension until June 1, 1942. He argued that he was healthy again, many men were being called back from retirement because of the war, and he had many projects yet to complete. In anticipation of his retirement, the Executive Board had voted to create the "West Special Fund, BSA" to pay off his home mortgage. The mortgage totaled $30,000 but Board member John Schiff (son of Mortimer) bought it for $20,545. The Board resolved to raise that money, buy the mortgage from Schiff, and present it to West as part of his retirement package. Board President Walter Head, Business Manager Earle Beckman, and West then solicited funds. They raised $21,670.

When Board members learned that over two-thirds of that money had come from BSA suppliers, they were quite upset about the perceived conflict of interest. When the question of West's pension was raised, they became even more upset. The proposal was to pay West his base salary for the rest of his life. In 1941 West received $20,000 in salary as Chief Scout Executive, $6,000 as Editor of Boys' Life, and an additional $5,000 as an "expense account." West did not have to itemize his expenses. In addition, the BSA General Fund paid all his transportation expenses as well as his club dues and bills. When he traveled, he insisted that the region or local council pay for meals and hotels. He also received an average of $2600 per year in reimbursement for "other expenses" which included "family illness" and "conference fees."[48] Board members speculated that these were expenses for his wife's travels and wondered about the tax liability for these payments to West. Some members also thought that West's lifestyle was extravagant and that he considered the BSA treasury as his own.[49]

The End of the Reign

Questions were raised about West's request that all members of the national staff organize troops in order to meet end-of-year recruiting goals, his billing distributors in advance in order to meet end-of-year financial goals, and his retaining his son's law firm for BSA business. The Board was also concerned about West's autocratic management style, the fact that the national staff was loyal to him rather than to the BSA, and his failure to identify a successor. The overriding concern, however, was West's refusal to accept the BSA's mandatory retirement age of 65. Board members agreed that all the other issues could be over-looked if only West would announce a date for his departure. A Special Committee of the Board met on February 17 and June 16, 1942 and resolved to recommend West's immediate retirement at the September 17 meeting of the full Board. Many Board members wrote to him urging him to go along with that recommendation. John Sherman Hoyt provided a good example in a July 18 letter addressed "Dear Jim:"

> I personally deprecate [sic] any action on your part that will mar your record of the past years for if you do not accept the committee decision, but decide to refer it to the September meeting of the National Executive Committee, the Board will confirm the recommendation of the committee and such action by the Board, in the eyes of the public would be equivalent to you having been discharged.
>
> If, now, on the other hand, you voluntarily resign, your retirement will be accorded by all the full honor due to your long and valued service.
>
> Please bear this in mind, Jim, that the sooner you submit your request for retirement, the happier it will be for you in the years to come. I am not happy at the outlook for your future if you put this off until the Board acts on your retirement.[50]

West refused and demanded to plead his case before the Board. A few hours prior to this meeting; however, a compromise was finally reached as West acknowledged the reality of the Board's voting to dismiss him. West would retire voluntarily, his mortgage would be paid off, he would receive an annual pension of $20,000, and he would receive the honorary title of "Chief Scout." The original suggestion had been to name West "Honorary Chief Scout Executive" and his successor "National Scout Executive;" however, the latter term seemed vague so it was decided to retain the title of "Chief Scout Executive" as head of the professional staff and resurrect the term "Chief Scout." As soon as the By-Laws were amended to include this office, West stepped down.

Chief Scout

Fisher summed up the transition very well:

> We admired the Chief Scout Executive in his personal message to the members of the Division of Operations as he indicated to them the likelihood that this occasion was the last conference which he would attend as the administrative officer of the Scout Movement. In words that were self-contained, restrained, unemotional, yet feelingly, he charged the men to go forward in building up the Scout Movement. We honored him for his spirit, his resolution, his kindliness, for we all know it meant the greatest transition in his life.[51]

On September 23, 1942 Board President Head issued the fateful press release, "Elections of Chief Scout and Chief Scout Executive." Head praised West for his brilliant and faithful service and awarded him the title "Chief Scout." While this was the title Baden-Powell had been given with respect, it was also the title that Seton received when he was given nothing meaningful to do. For West, it would be the latter.

West put the best spin he could on the situation. "I know of nothing that will give me greater pleasure than to see Scouting grow as it has never grown before, and I say to you in all sincerity, come what may, as long as my health permits, I am, through the office of Chief Scout, going to accept every opportunity that may come to me further to serve youth further to serve the boy. I know of no more effective way of serving the boy than through the program of the Boy Scouts of America."[52]

In his final column as Editor of *Boys' Life*, West wrote, "When I open my office as Chief Scout I shall continue to do my best to serve

youth and civilization through the program of the Boy Scouts of America
. . . I am truly grateful for all the help I have had over the years from so
many individuals and groups in my efforts 'to do my best.'"[50]

At the end of his tenure, West pointed to the statistics that defined
his Movement. Membership stood at 1,589,281 including 293,713 Cubs
and 1455 Scout Executives. There were over 51,000 Scout Troops
and Cub Packs in 541 councils. Twenty-eight national projects were
ongoing in cooperation with the government in the war effort. Official
distributors of uniforms and equipment included 1798 dealers and 349
agents. In the last year the national office had processed 2.8 million
pieces of incoming mail and 2.5 million pieces of outgoing mail as well
as 7.7 million magazines. The Boy Scouts of America had printed 42.5
million items ranging from mailing labels to handbooks. It was a huge
business of which West was justifiably proud.

On February 1, 1943 James E. West officially retired. On March
31 he was officially presented with his new insignia as Chief Scout at
a luncheon at the Biltmore Hotel in New York City. A photo of this
presentation was the last photograph of West to appear in *Boys' Life*
during his lifetime.

West's domination of the national office was so complete that there
was no obvious successor. The National Executive Board went outside
the professional ranks and chose Dr. Elbert K. Fretwell as the new
Chief Scout Executive and Editor of *Boys' Life*. Fretwell was Professor
of Education at Teachers College, Columbia University and had been
a member of the National Executive Board since 1933. He chaired the
Division of Program and the Committee on Education and was vice-
chair of the Division of Personnel and a member of the Editorial Board.
He had served as Dean of most of the National Executive Conferences.
His 1939 Silver Buffalo citation noted that he had been a "leader in
developing the modern public high school in America and in making it
a social institution." Both his sons were Scouts.

Fisher remained as Deputy Chief Scout Executive until January 4,
1944 when he retired and was named National Scout Commissioner,
Beard's old title. Fisher retained that title until he died in 1960. Vitalius
and Murphy stayed on as Fretwell's secretaries.

Fretwell did not write editorials or report on Good Turns and
awards in *Boys' Life* as West had done. West did remain on the masthead as "Chief Scout." Fretwell's annual reports were two hundred

pages shorter than West's. The program, however, did not immediately change.

The office of the new Chief Scout was in Room 6307 of the Chrysler Building at 405 Lexington Avenue, several blocks from National Headquarters. In addition to the title and the office, West was given an expense account, a secretary, and nothing meaningful to do. Perhaps he recalled what he had said in 1920: "Can there be more than one head in any organization?" West continued to take the train into the city every day and then read the newspapers. He was still called upon to speak, but wartime travel restrictions limited the distance that he could go. Perhaps some of those Eagle Scouts wrote to him. His biographical sketch in *Who's Who* listed the following duties: Advising Editor, *Parents' Magazine*, Board of Directors, Navy League of the United States, Board of Directors, National Information Bureau, Board of Trustees, Golden Rule Foundation, member New Rochelle Recreation Commission, and "cooperation" with the National Society of Crippled Children and Adults and the Ladies Auxiliary of the Veterans of Foreign Wars.[54] West also chaired the Board of Governors of the Westchester Country Club from 1944 until 1948. None of these duties compared to his previous responsibilities.

West had been elected as one of nine members of the International Committee (later called the World Bureau) in 1939. It was supposed to have been a two-year term, but no elections were held during the War. At the 1946 meeting in London, West was appointed chair of a subcommittee "to place the financial income of the Bureau on a more solid basis, so as to allow of development."[55] On that trip, he visited the British Scout Association and noted, with what must have been a great sense of irony, their acceptance of an executive staff. His suggestion that the Secretary of the International Committee be paid and not serve as a volunteer was adopted. At its formal meeting in 1947, the International Committee voted to expand to twelve members with staggered six-year terms, and Walter Head replaced West as the American representative.

West spent more time at home for the first time in his life. All of his children were now married, had children of their own, and lived close-by. The Wests had one of the first television sets in Westchester County and the grandchildren loved to visit. Sunday family dinners were served in New Rochelle or at Marion's house in New Jersey. Christmas was an important occasion. West always insisted on a family outing to select the tree and a trip to Macy's to suggest gifts.

When West attended the BSA's National Meeting in St. Louis in 1946, he had a personal aide as he always had. This man described him as a "lost soul," "crushed," and "an onlooker who couldn't handle not being the center of power."[56] West made his last major appearance at a Scouting function at the Eighth National Training Conference at Bloomington, Indiana on September 8, 1947. He spoke about the evolution of American Scouting, led by volunteers trained by professionals, in contrast to Britain where leaders were all volunteers "not burdened with the necessity of earning their own living." As an organization, the Boy Scouts of America was thriving, with one volunteer leader for every three boys. West praised the assembled executives for the work they were doing in making it possible for the volunteers to want to do their jobs and to make the Scouting program appealing to boys.[57]

West's health then deteriorated rapidly, probably due to Addison's disease and intestinal problems that were secondary to his long-standing tuberculosis. He finally became bedridden, helpless, and unable to organize and control the world around him. Privately he complained to his family that Scouting professionals, especially those whose careers he had nurtured, never came to visit him. The last man West had called a friend, General Theodore Roosevelt, had died of a heart attack at Normandy in June 1944. A nurse was hired to sit with West, but his grandchildren were told to be quiet and not to disturb him. His last words as he left home on the final trip to the hospital were, "I hurt." West died on May 15, 1948, one day short of his seventy-second birthday.

Final Tributes

Scouts provided the honor guard and H. Roe Bartle delivered the eulogy to "our beloved Chief" at the North Avenue Presbyterian Church in New Rochelle:

> No other man in this blessed democracy of ours has proved to be the great youth leader that Dr. James E. West proved himself to be decade after decade. He was true to every trust that was imposed in him - a trust

imposed in him by growing boys, by lads who wanted a code whereby they might develop into God-loving men who would serve their fellow-man and their country; a trust imposed in him by the men who were his colleagues and leaders in the Movement of Scouting . . .

I reflect upon the devotion which was his to his life's partner. Time after time in far-away places, as I would be by his side, he always wanted to call home to talk to that dear woman. He always inquired about the children . . .

The Chief loved his America. He loved it intensely, almost fanatically. He loved his America because it was our land that gave to him the opportunity to write such a great and indeed commanding record of life and living.[58]

President Truman sent a telegram to Mrs. West:

The death of your devoted husband brings to a close a career of great usefulness which will inspire American boys through long years to come. Dr. West had courage, faith, and vision - qualities which enabled him to overcome early handicaps that would have discouraged a less valiant spirit.

Boy Scouts of all ages and all Americans who believe in the future of the American boy bow in reverence to his memory. My heartfelt sympathy goes out to you and to all who mourn with you.[59]

The official BSA press response was more muted than the immediate tributes. *Boys' Life* ran only the second picture of the Chief Scout since his retirement. Under the heading, "The Chief Scout Takes the Long Trail," the article noted:

With the passing of Dr. James E. West the remarkable

story of a crippled orphan boy who rose to international fame because of his service to others came to a close. Despite his affliction, which resulted from an early illness, James E. West overcame many extraordinary handicaps to secure an education. His interest in boys and their welfare attracted the attention of President Theodore Roosevelt and it was through this presidential interest that Dr. West became the Chief Scout Executive of the Boy Scouts of America. He served in this capacity for thirty-two years and upon his retirement in 1943 he became the Chief Scout of the Movement. He served as Editor-in-Chief of *Boys' Life* and was always a vigorous champion of good reading for boys.[60]

Theodore Roosevelt, of course, had had nothing to do with West's becoming Chief Scout Executive. Ignorance of Scout history has a long tradition, but that does not excuse the error. The editors of *Boys' Life* may simply have decided that their boy readers no longer knew who West was and that Roosevelt had greater name recognition.

The *Scout Executive* ran part of Bartle's eulogy without comment. *Scouting* ran a full-page obituary, noting that "a great American has passed away." "It is hardly possible at this time to measure adequately the contribution of this great man to the Scout Movement and to the youth of the nation and the world. So many practices now universally accepted owed their origins to his vision that only the years can bring a full realization of his genius."[58] The magazine cited his ability to recruit and to organize as well as the registration plan, troop committees, local council structure, regional administration, and training for volunteers and professionals as major contributions. Many adult leaders would have remembered West, so this summary was more comprehensive and meaningful.

On May 19 the National Council adopted a resolution in tribute to West:

> By his abounding faith in himself and in the cause he loved, by his genius in organization, he piloted the movement from a few troops to an organization of magnificent proportions . . .

The End of the Reign

> Strongly individualistic in his views and ideas, he never wavered from, nor compromised, the basic principles of the movement; nor did he permit others to do so. He held tenaciously to its basic tenets. Advancement was never at the cost of lowered standards.[59]

The resolution went on to praise this lack of flexibility as West's greatest strength. It as also his greatest weakness.

Notes

[1] Beard Library of Congress (LOC) 110 5/20/39
[2] 3/08/38 letter in Edgar M. Robinson (EMR) Archives at Springfield College
[3] Beard LOC 209 undated
[4] 1/28/40 letter in BSA Archives
[5] 8/30/40 copy in BSA Archives
[6] 3/08/38 letter in EMR Archives
[7] Beard LOC 110 undated
[8] Levy, Harold. *Building a Popular Movement.* New York: Russell Sage Foundation, 1944 page 152
[9] Thirty-second Annual Report of the BSA page 24 ff
[10] Thirty-first Annual Report of the BSA page 23
[11] Thirty-second Annual Report of the BSA page 212
[12] Ibid page 53
[13] *Boys' Life* 10/41 page 30
[14] *Boys' Life* 10/39
[15] Letters collected by Terry Grove, personal communication
[16] *Boys' Life* 7/36 page 20
[17] Ibid page 19
[18] *Boys' Life* 2/37 page 16
[19] *Boys' Life* 8/36 page 19
[20] Thirty-first Annual Report of the BSA page 9
[21] *Boys' Life* 6/41 page 15
[22] Ibid
[23] 4/04/41 tribute in BSA Archives
[24] Emphasis his, BSA Archives
[25] Thirty-second Annual Report of the BSA page 87
[26] *Boys' Life* 9/41 page 6
[27] Copy in BSA Archives
[28] Beard LOC 12/19/40
[29] Quoted by Head in 9/23/42 announcement: "Election of Chief Scout and Chief Scout Executive"
[30] 10/29/40 letter in BSA Archives
[31] 11/29/40 letter in BSA Archives
[32] Thirty-first Annual Report of the BSA page 27
[33] "Helping Youth With A Song" BSA undated probably 1942
[34] BSA edition of the pledge, 1940
[35] Thirty-first Annual Report of the BSA page 95
[36] *Boys' Life* 11/40 page 44
[37] Dinner program page 10, BSA Archives

[38] *Scout Executive* 12/41 page 4

[39] Ibid page 1

[40] *Boys' Life* 1/42 page 3

[41] *Boys' Life* 3/42 page 3

[42] *Boys' Life* 5/42 page 3

[43] 2/07/42 Anniversary Week message to Scouts

[44] Levy, page 64

[45] "Pre-Ranger Program Training Manual" BSA 2/43 page 3

[46] Thirty-third Annual Report of the BSA page 10

[47] Thirty-second Annual Report of the BSA page 217

[48] Notes from undated (probably May 1942) interview of BSA Comptroller F. S. Pearse by Board member Frank A. Bean in Frank Weil Collection, Box 8 Folder 1 in American Jewish Archives

[49] 8/12/42 letter from Bean to Weil in Weil Archives Box 8 Folder 1

[50] Letter in Weil Archives Box 7 Folder 5

[51] *Scout Executive* 12/42 page 7

[52] Thirty-third Annual Report of the BSA page 55

[53] *Boys' Life* 3/43 page 3

[54] Copy in BSA Archives

[55] Lund, Richard. *The Boy Scout International Bureau.* Unpublished manuscript, 1971

[56] Don Green, personal communication

[57] Proceedings of the 8th NTC 1947 page 268

[58] *Scout Executive* 6/48 page 1

[59] Copy in BSA Archives

[60] *Boys' Life* 7/48 page 3

[61] *Scouting* 6-7/48 page 2

[62] As quoted in 1948 Annual Report page 52

Chapter 8

Afterword

Personal and professional deconstruction of the West legacy began shortly after his death. His will, filed in Westchester County Surrogate's Court on May 24, 1948, left everything to his wife. The house was appraised at $35,000 and he had over $73,000 in life insurance, as well as stock in the Country Club and personal property. He also had a mortgage, so that the net value of his estate was only $89,630.54. (That's $722,000 in 2005 dollars.) One item on the appraisal was an "oil painting signed Albert Rose, family portrait of gentleman in boy scout executive's uniform, 40" x 30" in gilt frame - no value."[1]

Mrs. West stayed in the New Rochelle home after her husband died, but Perry Crandall, an old high school admirer, contacted her and they began to correspond. In 1951 she went to the convent next door and asked if the sisters wanted to buy the house. They did. She sold it, married Crandall, and moved to Jupiter, Florida. The house on North Avenue was soon transferred to the Irish Christian Brothers and is now part of Iona College.

Those family members who thought that "Nana" had made a mistake when she remarried thought that she was unhappy in Florida. Those who thought she had reached for her dream thought that she was happier there than she had been with West. After her brother Charlie died, she moved her sister-in-law to a near-by community. When "Nana" died in 1959, Marion had her body returned (some say "kidnapped Nana") to New York for burial next to her father. Finally, after eleven years, Arthur then removed a wooden marker and put a stone monument on the graves. He got the emblems wrong as two British fleur-de-lis and not American Scout badges were carved into the stone. In 1960, on the fiftieth anniversary of the incorporation of the Boy Scouts of America, a local troop laid a wreath on West's grave. Arthur West was present. It was the first and last James E. West pilgrimage and was not reported in the Scout literature.

Arthur was apparently the only child to make regular visits to the cemetery. Some in the family say that he missed the financial support more than he missed his father. He was not very successful in the practice of law and always seemed to be borrowing money.

Marion was the child most like her father. She and her husband were in the real estate business in New Jersey. She was also a politician. She campaigned for Goldwater in 1964 and was elected to the New Jersey Assembly, where she rose to the position of Speaker. New Jersey has no Lieutenant Governor, so when the Governor is out of state, the Speaker acts as Governor. Marion took great pride in her role as "Governor for a day." She was the only West child to be active in Scouting as an adult, first as a Den Mother and later as a member of the Executive Board and Vice-President of the Bergen County Council.

Helen attended the New York School of Interior Design and worked for Lord and Taylor, a department store. She co-founded the Bedford (New York) Christian School.

Bob graduated from Princeton and the Columbia College of Physicians and Surgeons and practiced pediatrics in Mount Kisko, New York for many years.

Many of the children picked up parental habits. "What did you do for God and family today" was a common dinner theme. There has been a significant family problem with alcohol. No one has accused West of being an alcoholic. While it would not be a surprise in view of his chronic pain, it does not appear to have been the case. The more likely candidate for the origin of what is now considered to be a genetic predisposition to alcoholism would be West's father, who had gone off and left a wife and young son in Washington. This would also suggest that West had even more self-discipline in resisting an ongoing temptation to use alcohol to reduce his chronic pain.

Why do the Boy Scouts minimize West's role in their history? It could be a collective "institutional memory" where people who never knew West have heard stories passed down from previous generations and think of him negatively. The legend may have grown like the London fog in 1909. It may simply be that the guardian of the records is right "to protect our history from modern interpretation," or rather, to protect the fictionalized history from honest interpretation. Some BSA history, like racism, is bad. Some stories, such as Boyce lost in a fog, have been reported incorrectly for so long that a correction would now be embarrassing.

James E. West was a difficult man to like. He was an autocrat and a chauvinist. Dan Beard was a deceitful back-stabber, Seton a "hippie" idealist, and Boyce a racist. If we look closely at West, then we see him and his contemporaries in Scouting as the flawed individuals that they were; however, each was a man of his time and modern interpreters should realize this. Perhaps, to look at West and these contemporaries as real people would detract from the perception of idealism that the organization is trying to promote.

West wanted desperately to rise above his humble origins. He had experienced childhood abandonment, humiliation, and chronic illness and limped through life in an organization that promoted physical fitness. He sought power, control, and recognition, and he achieved these goals. He received awards and testimonials as well as recognition by presidents and movie stars and millions of Scouts and leaders. He wielded immense power. He was forceful, egotistical, and tolerated fools badly. He demanded uncompromising obedience and loyalty. He established a bureaucracy and management style that still endures. He was also the right man for the job, as any less powerful individual could not have stood up to Beard and Seton and would have seen the organization fragment around him. He sincerely believed that he did it all for "the boy."

The non-profit organizational structure that West pioneered - influential board members focus on vision and finance and leave the day-to-day operation to the "professionals" - is nearly universal today. West created a profession in his own image and framed it in terms of service to others. Today's organization may reject him as a person, but it retains the structural heritage that he pioneered. In 1948 *Scouting* magazine had predicted that West would be remembered as a "genius." The Boy Scouts of America appears to be determined that the details not be remembered at all.

Afterword

The Legacy

Some aspects of Scouting were to change but others were not. Fretwell served as a "caretaker" Chief for five years, and his retirement signaled several of the changes that would occur.

> This month [September 1948] *Boys' Life* welcomed Arthur A. Schuck formerly Scout Executive of the Los Angeles Area Council to the position of Chief Scout Executive of the Boy Scouts of America. He succeeds Dr. Elbert K. Fretwell who retired from active service and accepted the honorary post of Chief Scout, the office filled until his death by Dr. James E. West. The new Chief Scout Executive has a rich experience in Scouting and knows boys, serving as a Scoutmaster and a Scout Commissioner before he entered Scouting professionally.[2]

The article did not state that, prior to his five years in Los Angeles, Schuck had spent nearly twenty years of his professional career as West's Director of Operations. Every Chief Scout Executive since Schuck has come up through the professional ranks. Fretwell was the last Executive to become Chief Scout in retirement, and Schuck was the last to receive and use an honorary doctorate and receive the Silver Buffalo while in office.

Amory Houghton of Corning Glass, had replaced Walter Head as President of the National Executive Board at the Annual Meeting in 1946. Although present, West was not invited to speak at the testimonial dinner for Head. As tenure of the Chief Scout Executive was to be limited, so was the tenure of the Board President. No future president was to serve as long as Head.[3]

Two programs that West had never embraced became national in scope in 1948. Woodbadge training began at Schiff Scout Reservation and the Order of the Arrow was now active in 367 Councils. That same year the Scouts and Cubs gave up their breeches and knickers in favor of long pants. (A new Scout uniform cost $10.65)[4] In 1947 West's "Cubs" had become "Cub Scouts" and the age at which a boy could join was lowered to eight. The Boy Scout entry age was lowered to eleven and the Senior program, now called "Exploring" began at fourteen. (This particular Exploring program was discontinued in 1959.) In 1950 the Achievement Scout program ended and the issue of advancement for handicapped scouts was then handled on an individual basis. Also in 1950, the name of Franklin K. Mathiews, the old "book physician," was finally dropped from the masthead of *Boys' Life*. He was then eighty-two years old and had not reviewed a book or movie in years.

National Headquarters moved from New York City to a New Brunswick, New Jersey campus in October 1954. National Supply Service, the National Museum, and the Augustus International Scout House were also located there. Schiff was nearby. The campus was closed and National Headquarters moved again to Irving, Texas in October 1979, ostensibly to be nearer a major airport. Schiff Scout Reservation was closed and sold at that time. The original twelve regions were consolidated to six in 1972 and then to four in 1992. The 541 local councils that West presided over in 1941 have merged into slightly more than 300 today. Major promotions are made from outside a council so that loyalty remains up the chain of command rather than to a community. West dominated his organization, but since his retirement, the Chief Scout Executive has become essentially a "faceless" position. Few Scouters and almost none of the general public could name the incumbent. There is no charismatic figure in the program. Dan Beard embodied traditional patriotic values, but he has been forgotten. Bill Hillcourt promoted traditional programs, but no successor was identified after he died in 1992. Efficient, impersonal management prevails. West would be proud.

West's vision of "traditional values" and a religious emphasis continues. In fact, hierarchical, male-dominated religions such as the Mormons, Roman Catholics, and Southern Baptists are the most likely to embrace the Scouting program. In many ways, the "Movement" has been captured by the organizations it was meant to serve and reflects a shift to the right in American society. "Timeless values," not innovations have prevailed.

Innovations were tried once. In the early 1960s there was a study by the University of Michigan entitled, "Is Scouting in tune with the times?"[5] The answer was "no," and the program changed dramatically. Skill awards replaced the old advancement requirements, diversity appeared in the literature, and everyone wore red berets. Perhaps someone should have consulted the McKenzie statuette beforehand because the changes were unsuccessful in attracting more boys and a "traditional program" returned. At the same time, there was a campaign called "Boypower '76." The goal was to recruit one boy in three to become a Scout. Conceptually it looked a lot like the Ten Year Program instituted by West, and it failed just as quickly and even more spectacularly, as some Executives were discovered to have fabricated boys and even troops in order to meet their goals. These failures were interpreted to mean that being "in tune with the times" was wrong. Tradition seemed best and the next slogan would be "America is returning to the values that Scouting never left."

"Boypower" became a good example of a program that was organizationally rather than mission driven, despite rhetoric to the contrary. This top-down concept is called "management by objective." The national office sets an objective, such as the number of new Scouts or dollars needed. The goal is divided among the regions who divide it among the councils. Councils divide it among districts, who then divide it among troops, all in the name of providing citizenship training and character development to more youngsters. If it were truly "all about program," then there would be no need for the Chief Scout Executive's Winners' Circle, Quality Councils and Districts, the National President's Marketing Award for Excellence, the National Endowment Achievement Award or professional recognitions for recruiting and fund-raising.

The Boy Scouts of America is still trying to find a "senior" program that holds the interest of teen-agers. School-based and vocationally-oriented programs are currently keeping up the number of registered adolescents. A new program called Tiger Cubs was introduced in 1981. West could never have imagined six or seven-year-old first graders being "Scouts." The organization is no longer at war with the Girl Scouts, and, in fact, "senior" Scout programs have been co-ed for many years. The entire Camp Fire program went co-ed in 1975 after failed discussions with the Boy Scouts about merging those two organizations.

West clearly felt that women had their place, preferably at home with the children, and certainly not at work as Scout executives. While women have been admitted to the executive ranks for years, the glass ceiling is still low. In July 2002, sixteen percent of Scouting professionals were women, most in entry-level positions.[6] Very few of the current

300 plus local Council Executives are women, and service as a Council Executive is a necessary step prior to a move onto the national stage.

West made no public statement about sexual orientation, but the present position of the Boy Scouts of America is consistent with his standards: believe in God, wear the uniform correctly, and set a proper example. Like German Scoutmasters in 1917, "poor role models" are not tolerated. This position prevents the loss of conservative sponsoring institutions. A real paradox in the trend toward conservatism and the threat to cancel charters of local councils that maintain a "don't ask, don't tell" policy has been the "politically correct" and racially sensitive issue of the current renaming of councils and campsites that were originally named for Confederate generals such as Robert E. Lee, A. P. Hill, and Stonewall Jackson. This is reminiscent of the "rules" conflict of the 1920's. The structure was "democratic" so that local councils could separate the races according to local custom but not democratic enough to "avoid participation in controversial topics" and not confront women who smoked. It has always been difficult to strike the right balance

West's contributions have been sanitized and summarized. "He was the first Chief Scout Executive and architect of the largest and most effective youth organization in the world."[7] That is as much as people need to know. Most National Jamborees since 1969 have had a James E. West campsite. From 1950 through 1971, the Ladies Auxiliary of the Veterans of Foreign Wars presented the "James E. West Award," a $500 college scholarship to a Scout for service to conservation. Annual reports contain no information as to why it was discontinued. There is a James E. West Fellowship award for those who contribute $1000 or more to local council endowment funds; however, this is now an "entry level" award and is overshadowed by the "Founders' Circle" and "1910 Society" levels: $25,000 Ernest Thompson Seton, $100,000 Daniel Carter Beard, $500,000 Theodore Roosevelt, and $1,000,000 Waite Phillips. Beard would be pleased to think that he was four times as valuable as Seton and one hundred times as valuable as West.

West's uniform was on display at the National Museum in Kentucky, but the Scout history video that played continuously did not mention his name and even suggested that Baden-Powell had made his own arrangements to meet with Presidents Taft and Roosevelt during his 1912 tour. Realistically, none of the Founders of Scouting, with the possible exception of Baden-Powell, are household names. There is no badge for the study of history. Boys still become Scouts to have fun, not to build their character. National policy debates are generally irrelevant to those working directly with youth. Why care about the past?

If the Boy Scouts of America had studied its history, it might have avoided some mistakes such as "Boypower." Despite resistance, blacks have entered the program, women have entered the program, and gays may enter the program.

"Those who cannot remember the past are condemned to repeat it."—Santayana

"The only history we don't know is the history we haven't read." –Harry Truman

Afterword

Notes

---

[1] file # 1948-1224
[2] *Boys' Life* 9/48 page 3
[3] "Twenty years of Service: Tributes to Walter W. Head" BSA 1946
[4] In 2005 a new uniform cost $98.90
[5] Yankelovich, David. "Is Scouting in Tune With The Times?" BSA 1968
[6] *Scouting* 1-2/2003 page 24
[7] Big League Card

References

Baden-Powell, Robert S. S. *The Matabele Campaign 1896*. London: Methuen, 1897.

_____. *Scouting for Boys*. London: Pearson, 1908.

Beard, Daniel C. *Hardly a Man is Now Alive*. New York: Doubleday, Doran, 1939.

Berg, A. Scott. *Lindbergh*. New York: Berkley, 1999.

Block, Nelson. *A Thing of the Spirit: The Life of E. Urner Goodman*. Irving, Texas: Boy Scouts of America, 2000.

Boyce, William D. *Illustrated Australia and New Zealand*. Chicago: Rand McNally Press, 1922.

_____. *Illustrated Africa*. Chicago: Rand McNally Press, 1925.

Boy Scouts of America.

    Boys' Life. 1911-1948, 2001

    Scouting. 1913-1948, 1960, 2003

    Scout Executive. 1920-1948 (published as *Scout Administrator*. 1935-1936)

    Annual Report of the Boy Scouts of America. 1910-1948

    Proceedings of National Conferences for Scout Executives 1922, 1924, 1926, 1928, 1936, 1939, 1947.

    Community Boy Leadership: A Manual for Scout Executives. 1921.

    Scouting With a Neckerchief. 1927.

    The Father and Son Idea and Scouting. 1928.

    Historic Statement of the Boy Scouts of America. Mimeo. 1930.

    The Troop Program and Scouting Tenure. 1934.

    Jamboree-ing in Washington: What Scouts will want to see and do. 1937.

    Scouting for Rural Boys. 1938.

    Election of Chief Scout and Chief Scout Executive. 9/23/42.

    Pre-Ranger Training Program. 1943.

    America's Answer. Undated but probably 1938.

    Helping Youth With a Song. Undated but probably 1942.

Curtis, H. S. "The Boy Scouts." *Educational Review* December 1915.

Dizer, John. *Tom Swift, The Bobbsey Twins, and Other Heroes of American Juvenile Literature.* Lewiston, NY: Edwin Mellon Press, 1997.

Douglas, Richard, Martin, David, & Oliver, Douglas. *Three Boy Scouts in Africa.* New York: G P Putnam's Sons, 1928.

Goodman, E. Urner. "James E. West as I knew him." *Now and Then.* Winter, 1971.

Grant, James. *Boys' Book of Single Shot Rifles.* New York: Wm. Morrow & Co, 1967.

Gornick, James. *James Edward West: A Servant of Youth.* Unpublished manuscript, 1973.

Handbook: Boy Rangers of America. New York, 1925.

Hillcourt, William. *Baden-Powell: Two Lives of a Hero.* New York: G P Putnam's Sons, 1964.

_____. *Norman Rockwell's World of Scouting.* New York: Henry N. Abrams, 1977.

Hofstader, Richard. *The Progressive Movement 1910-1915.* Englewood Cliffs, NJ: Prentice Hall, 1963.

Levy, Harold. *Building a Popular Movement.* New York: Russell Sage Foundation, 1944.

Lund, Richard. *The Boy Scout International Bureau.* Unpublished manuscript, 1971.

Macleod, David. *Building Character in the American Boy.* Madison: University of Wisconsin Press, 1983.

Malatzky, David. Summer Camp! New York: Greater New York Councils, BSA, 2002.

McGuire, Paul. "Scout Rangers Handbook, BSA" Iowa City: Iowa City Area Council, BSA, mimeo, date unknown.

Money, John. The Destroying Angel. Buffalo: Prometheus, 1985.

Monroe, Keith. "Jim West: Scouting's Gruff Genius." *Scouting* November-December 1974.

Murray, William. *As He Journeyed.* New York: Association Press. 1929.

_____. *The History of the Boy Scouts of America.* New York: BSA, 1937.

Oursler, Will. *The Boy Scout Story.* Garden City, NY: Doubleday & Co. 1955.

Petterchak, Janice. *Lone Scout: W. D. Boyce and American Boy Scouting.* Legacy Press, 2003.

Phillips, John. *Selling America: The Boy Scouts of America in the Progressive Era, 1910-1921.* Unpublished Masters Thesis, University of Maine, 2001.

Pote, Harold. *Fifty Years of Scouting and Its Pioneers.* Printed privately, undated.

Robinson, Edgar M. *Recollections of the Early Days of the Boy Scouts of America.* Unpublished manuscript in Springfield College Library, 1948.

_____. *The Early Years.* New York: Association Press, 1950.

Russell, James E. "Scouting Education." *Educational Review* June 1917.

Salomon, Julian. *Three Great Scouts and a Lady.* Unpublished manuscript. 1976.

Seton, Ernest Thompson. *Trail of an Artist Naturalist.* New York: Scribners, 1940.

Shaver, W. Waldo. *A Pioneer's Journal of Scouting Stories.* Printed privately, 1977.

Siple, Paul. *A Boy Scout With Byrd.* New York: G P Putnam's Sons, 1931.

Stearns, Myron. "Boys Will Be Scouts." *American Magazine.* June 1927.

Thirty Years of Service: Tributes to James E. West. New York: Carey Press, 1941.

Twenty Years of Service: Tributes to Walter W. Head. BSA 1946.

Trine, Ralph . *The Best of Ralph Waldo Trine.* New York: Bobbs-Merrill, 1957.

Wagner, Carolyn. *The Boy Scouts of America: A Model and a Mirror of American Society.* Unpublished PhD dissertation, Johns Hopkins University, 1978.

Webb, Gerald. *Tuberculosis.* New York: Hoeber, 1936.

Welch, J. E. "George J. Fisher: Leader of Youth" *Journal of Health, Physical Education, and Recreation.* May 1968.

West, James E. "The real Boy Scout." *Leslie's Weekly* April 18, 1912.

_____. "Stumbling into Citizenship" BSA 1920.

_____. *Making the Most of Yourself.* New York: Appleton-Century, 1941.

_____. *The Lone Scout of the Sky.* New York: BSA, 1927.

West, James E. (editor) *The Boy Scout's Book of True Adventure.* New York: G P Putnam's Sons, 1931.

West, James E. & Hillcourt, William. *The 1933 Scout Jamboree Book.* New York: G P Putnam's Sons, 1933.

West, James E. & Lamb, Peter. *The Boys' Book of Honor.* New York: H. Revell Co., 1931.

_____. *He-Who-Sees-In-The-Dark*. New York: Brewer, Warren & Putnam, 1932.

Whitmore, Allan. *Beard, Boys and Buckskins.* Unpublished PhD dissertation, Northwestern University, 1970.

Williams, J. Harold. *Scout Trail 1910-1962.* Providence, RI: Narragansett Council, BSA 1964.

Wo-He-Lo: The Camp Fire History. Campfire Inc. 1980.

Index